JAMES MICHAEL
CURLEY

JAMES MICHAEL
CURLEY

A Short Biography with Personal Reminiscences

by WILLIAM M. BULGER

Edited by Robert J. Allison

COMMONWEALTH EDITIONS
Carlisle, Massachusetts

FOR

CARL THAYER

Library of Congress Cataloging-in-Publication Data
Bulger, William M.
  James Michael Curley : a short biography with personal reminiscences /
by William M. Bulger ; edited by Robert J. Allison.
     p. cm.
  Includes bibliographical references and index.
  ISBN 978-1-933212-75-3 (alk. paper)
  1. Curley, James Michael, 1874–1958. 2. Governors–Massachusetts—
Biography. 3. Mayors—Massachusetts—Boston—Biography. 4. Massa-
chusetts—Politics and government—1865–1950. 5. Irish
Americans—Massachusetts—Politics and government. I. Allison, Robert J.
II. Title.

  F70.C85B855 2009
  328.73092—dc22
  [B]

                                              2009002818

First published in hardcover, 2009

Front cover photo: Boston Public Library
Cover design by John Barnett / 4 Eyes Design
Printed in the United States of America

Commonwealth Editions is an imprint of Applewood Books, Inc.,
Carlisle, Massachusetts 01741.
Visit us on the web at www.commonwealtheditions.com.

CONTENTS

PREFACE

James Michael Curley remains Boston's most colorful, controversial, and interesting public figure. Rascal King or Mayor of the Poor? From his first election to the Boston Common Council in 1899 to his final race for mayor in 1955, Curley dominated Boston's political life as no other individual has. Thirty years after he left office, the city built two statues of him, and forty years after his death, a Boston rock band recorded a song about him. Curley still looms large in Boston's history.

William Bulger also looms large in Boston's history. First elected to the Massachusetts House of Representatives in 1960, Bulger in his initial weeks in office heard John F. Kennedy's stirring call to be men of courage, judgment, integrity, and dedication, a call that he heeded over the next forty-five years in public life. Elected to the state senate in 1970, Bulger served as that body's president for eighteen years, before his appointment by a Republican governor to lead the University of Massachusetts. As state senator from South Boston, Bulger hosted the annual St. Patrick's Day Breakfast, an uproarious political spectacle in the tradition of James Michael Curley.

In this book Bulger demonstrates the persistence of James Michael Curley's influence on Boston's political culture. Bulger may have been a political disciple of Curley, but his intellectual influences are Dr. Samuel Johnson and Father Carl Thayer; the latter introduced Bulger as a college student to the ancient Greeks and Romans. William Bulger reminisces about James Michael Curley from the unique perspective of a lifelong student of history and a lifelong political player. He reveals much about Curley and the unique political culture in which Curley flourished.

Robert J. Allison, editor
Boston, Massachusetts

1

THAT MAN CURLEY

I got out of the army on September 7, 1955, and was coming out of Andrew Square Station in South Boston three weeks later when I saw my friend and childhood neighbor from Logan Way, Joe Moakley. He was holding a sign for John Powers, candidate for mayor.

"Bill, I hope you'll be with John Powers for mayor," he said. Joe then was a state representative; Powers was our state senator. For the first time in my life I would be able to vote in a mayoral election, and I told him no, that this might be the only chance I would have to vote for James Michael Curley. Curley was on the ballot—he was eighty-one and did not have a prayer of winning. Of course, Joe Moakley could not understand that kind of sentimentality.

Curley was my earliest political hero. His days of officeholding were well behind him—he had first been elected to the Common Council more than fifty years earlier, and though he had been mayor of Boston four times (1914–1918, 1922–1926, 1930–1934, 1946–1950), congressman twice (1911–1914, 1943–1946), and governor of Massachusetts once (1935–1937), he had been defeated in 1949 and 1951 and was viewed as a political boss, a "rascal king," a buccaneer, and, according to his critics, totally unworthy of the public trust. I saw him as a man of courage (which he was) with a rich sense of humor (which he had) and a gift for entertaining bombast. He was certainly—in my mind—a man of greater virtue than his foes. That he could survive and still render such enormous public service was enough for me. I gave Curley my first vote for mayor of Boston as a way of keeping faith with the past.

Four years earlier, on primary night 1951, I had ventured downtown to the Hotel Brunswick, a venerable institution now, like Curley, long gone. A bedraggled lot had gathered. There was Charlie MacGillivray, whom I had known as a neighbor back on O'Callaghan Way, recipient of the Congressional Medal of Honor. He had left an arm behind on a battlefield in Europe. There was Jimmy Coffey, city councilor from East Boston, who had disgraced himself with a bit of ill-timed candor, answering an ethics question by saying, "I'll take a buck," and known thereafter as James "I'll take a buck" Coffey.

And in came James Michael Curley, his life shadowed now by grief and defeat. He had finished second in the primary, thirty

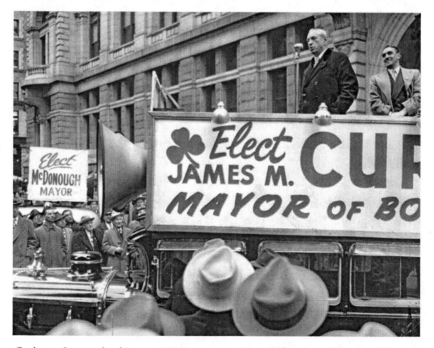

Curley as I remember him—castigating an opponent on the stump. (Courtesy Boston Public Library)

thousand votes behind John B. Hynes, who had beaten him in 1949. To many in the city he represented a past best forgotten.

I will never forget the look of him in his brown suit as he walked past me, his jaw a bit slack. He had survived the primary election, but he was so far behind Hynes that there was no chance that he would ever again taste victory. A few days later he would in fact suspend his campaign. But that night, after he patiently waited for the microphones to be adjusted, he came alive with a strident speech that I can still hear coming from that distant and desolate room. "Like John Paul Jones on the deck of the burning *Bon Homme Richard,* asked if he was prepared to surrender, he answered, 'Surrender? We've just begun to fight!'"

The crowd, men and women well along in years, was not watching the last gasps of a dying era. These people were so touched by the fire and familiar confidence in the Curley voice, so swept up in the wonder of his vision, that I thought we were going to march on City Hall.

One year after that primary night, in September 1952, as a freshman at Boston College, I enrolled in Father Carl Thayer's course in ancient Greek language and literature. Father Thayer admired most the men of action—Demosthenes, Thucydides, Cicero. The philosophers, he said, were always spinning theories. What did they really do? The men of action, the politicians, were the heroes, though they came out looking the worse for it.

Thayer assigned us to write a paper on a subject of our own choosing. After my encounter with Demosthenes' Oration on the Crown, given in the face of his own defeat, I chose to write about James Michael Curley's 1946 trial and 1947 imprisonment for mail fraud. Curley had not actually committed mail fraud; the case against him was tortuous and convoluted. President Roosevelt (though he may have wanted to get Curley) had told Congressman John McCormack that Curley had nothing to worry about, and Curley's longtime political adversary, Senator David Walsh, thought the charges were meaningless. Why was there such an effort to get him?

Here is the case. In the summer of 1941 Curley had allowed an unscrupulous character, James G. Fuller, to use Curley's name in a scheme to secure government defense contracts for his specious "Engineers Group." After Fuller's checks bounced, Curley severed his ties to Fuller, who continued his illicit schemes to defraud the government.

During the war Senator Harry Truman of Missouri investigated fraudulent wartime contracts and discovered Fuller's Engineers Group as one of the culprits. In 1944 Attorney General Anthony Drexel Biddle learned that Curley's name was on the Engineers Group letterhead. Truman knew Curley's involvement was negligible, but the Justice Department indicted Curley.

Though Curley during his long career had been accused of many illicit acts, the "crime" for which he went to jail was not clearly criminal: he had allowed an unscrupulous man to use his name in 1941; by the time Curley was indicted in 1946, that man had long since been jailed for writing bad checks, one of which was to Curley himself. Curley's involvement with the Engineers Group was inconsequential—certainly it was not on a par with the malfeasance of some wartime contractors, as exemplified in Arthur Miller's sobering play *All My Sons*—and yet Curley was pursued as though he were the mastermind, *because* he was James Michael Curley. Joseph Dinneen, Curley's biographer in 1949, believed that the public perception of Curley as a demagogue, a charlatan, a rogue, or, as a recent biographer calls him, a rascal king, was enough to convict him in the court of public opinion and in a court of law.

What intrigued me, as a freshman at Boston College, was that in order to get someone who was deemed "bad," the prosecutors themselves felt free to behave badly, even illegally. In a system that allowed for this type of zeal (which Justice Brandeis had warned about: "Experience should teach us to be most on our guard to protect liberty when the government's purposes are beneficent"; men will guard their freedom against evildoers, but the "greatest dangers to liberty lurk in insidious encroachment by men of zeal, well-meaning but without understanding"), who would be safe? And who would police the police themselves?

I recall that Father Thayer invited me to read my paper to my classmates. That course began for me a relationship with Father Thayer that would last until the end of his life, in 1990. It also initiated a greater interest in politics and a formal engagement with James Michael Curley, whose spirit animated political life for decades in Boston.

My Curley paper was provocative. Many of my classmates were sons of the suburbs, young men whose families would not have looked with favor on James Michael Curley. Curley to them represented a bygone era, the city boss, a corrupt and incorrigible urban charlatan. I had a different, more favorable impression.

My own memories of Curley—and I suspect the memories many hold of him—are positive. I am not going to disturb the memories, or to replace them with the sterile certainty of fact. The question is: How and why did Curley have such a hold, for so many years, over so many of the people of Boston, and why does his life story, more so than that of any of his Massachusetts contemporaries, remain interesting, even though he has been supplanted in many ways by John F. Kennedy? Could you imagine a public fascination with Henry Cabot Lodge, the senator and scholar? Or Calvin Coolidge, who became president? Massachusetts in the twentieth century produced four Speakers of the U.S. House of Representatives, two presidents of the United States, countless national candidates, Cabinet secretaries, ambassadors, jurists, novelists, and other dignitaries. But only one James Michael Curley.

Curley became a curious public persona, to be observed and enjoyed as a remarkable political spectacle. Only Bostonians could understand this anomaly, a man who had been sent to jail and who would time after time gain the confidence of the Boston electorate. It was a puzzle to outsiders. Bostonians claimed to understand and were pleased by the insider status that such understanding assured for them.

The Belgian Military Mission visits Boston, August 1917. Left to right: General Mathieu LeClercq of Belgium, the Belgian consul E. S. Mansfield, Lieutenant Governor Calvin Coolidge, Baron Ludovic Moncheur, former president Theodore Roosevelt, Curley, and Governor Samuel McCall. Curley and Roosevelt, the only men smiling, always found their way into the center of the picture. (Courtesy College of the Holy Cross)

It was fun to rejoice in his success. He was not to be carefully scrutinized. His critics were at that task incessantly. His foes' frenzied fulminations were worth the price of keeping him in office. It was an act of defiance against those who had the means to broadcast their point of view. The people of Harlem evidenced this same good spirit in their support of Congressman Adam Clayton Powell. "And the more you do not like him, the more we do. What do we owe you, anyway? He has shown his understanding of what our concerns are. You are indifferent to us and to our concerns until you wish us to do as you tell us to do."

For Curley himself, this, his second stint in jail, ended on the day before Thanksgiving in 1947. President Truman pardoned Curley, after each of the Commonwealth's congressmen petitioned him to do so. Every congressman, that is, except for John

F. Kennedy. When Curley had left Congress in 1945 to run once more for mayor of Boston, Kennedy had run for and won his seat, representing East Boston, the North End, and Charlestown, as well as the outlying suburb of Cambridge. Now Kennedy refused to sign the petition requesting the presidential pardon for the old mayor (Curley then was seventy-three). Some pundits have suggested that Kennedy's hard-heartedness derived from his ambition—how would it look in the rest of the provinces to be tainted by empathy for the old scoundrel? It may have reflected the fact that Kennedy was in many ways more like the young men I encountered in my freshman year at Boston College.

But I sometimes think that Kennedy was acting in this instance not like an up-and-coming politician or a callous son of privilege. He was acting like a politician with a long memory. Curley had tangled with both of Kennedy's grandfathers—the East Boston ward leader Patrick Joseph Kennedy and the North End boss John F. "Honey Fitz" Fitzgerald. Curley in 1914 had humiliated Fitzgerald, then at the height of his career, having just completed a successful term as mayor of the city; Curley drove Honey Fitz out of the race for reelection and thereafter drove the old man out of politics (about which more later). Young Jack Kennedy may have had an eye on his political future, but the personal grudge of Honey Fitz was the more likely basis for Kennedy's action. Fitz had been the favorite of the Kennedy boys, and adoption of the old man's grudges would have been a sign of affection and respect.

Kennedy notwithstanding, Curley's stint in the Danbury penitentiary, and the tumultuous greeting on his arrival at South Station on that November day in 1947, showed that many Bostonians felt a loyalty of a certain kind toward the old man.

You can see the source of this deep loyalty even more clearly in Curley's first jail term, in 1904. (Since the one fact everyone—native Bostonian or casual visitor—knows about Curley is that he had been in jail, I will get this part of the story out of the way in this chapter.) Curley then was running for the Board of Aldermen, the "upper house" of the City Council (in those days Boston had a seventy-five-member Common Council and a twelve-member Board of Aldermen). Curley had already served on the Common Council and in the state legislature; he and his colleague Thomas F. Curley—no relation—had made their Tammany organization a powerhouse in Roxbury's Ward 17. The key to the Curleys' success was in finding work for their constituents. Two of them, Bartholomew Fahey and James Hughes, wanted to be letter carriers. Curley could tell they had the feet for the job, but unfortunately their heads were not crammed with the kind of knowledge required to pass a civil service exam. James Curley and Thomas Curley were inspired to take the test for Fahey and Hughes, who thus would obtain gainful employment and be able to support their growing families. The Curleys passed the exams, but a court officer from a rival political organization spotted them. The two Curleys were arrested for attempting to defraud the government of the United States.

Federal Judge James Lowell was not impressed with the defense that the Curleys were not trying to defraud the government, but merely trying to get jobs for Fahey and Hughes. Curley argued that the law allowed proxies to represent men taking the exam; it did not specifically forbid the proxies to take the exam. Judge Lowell thought this a subtle technicality, and he sentenced the two Curleys to spend sixty days in the Charles Street Jail. Lowell chastised them for their fraud and for waging a political campaign from his courtroom and then from the Charles Street Jail.

After a year of unsuccessful appeals, Curley's jail term began on November 7, 1904. The regular Democratic organization and the Good Government Association thought they had heard the last of him. But as the journalist Joseph Dinneen later wrote, from a poor case in court Curley fashioned a good case before the public. He said he had intentionally broken an unjust law. A rich man could afford to hire all the assistance he needed, but a poor man was denied representation. Furthermore, and more plainly, Curley had gone to jail not because he had enriched himself, but for trying to help another. "He did it for a friend" became Curley's slogan. If he was willing to go to jail to help Fahey and Hughes, what might he do for you?

"I helped a friend," Curley said in 1930, looking back on this early campaign. "It would have been different if there were money involved—if I had been paid for what I did. There was not. A friend needed my help, and I gave it. I think that most people, these days, are willing to see it as I do myself—a mistake of my early life."

Much to the surprise of all but themselves, on election day in 1903, after being convicted of fraud, James Michael Curley and Tom Curley beat the regular Democratic and the Good Government Association's candidates by a vote of three to one. In 1904, while serving their sentences, the Curleys were easily reelected.

Curley's time in jail was well spent. The Charles Street Jail at that time had a well-stocked library, and Curley, with an enforced stretch of leisure for the first time in his life, read through every book in it and then ordered more from the newly completed Boston Public Library. He read voraciously—Shakespeare, *The Life of Thomas Jefferson,* John Bunyan's *Pilgrim's Progress* (which he particularly relished, as Bunyan had written that classic while he was imprisoned). After his stint in jail, Curley's speeches and public utterances had many more allusions to great literature and quotes from Shakespeare and other classics. You get the impression that when Curley read Shakespeare, he was looking for ammunition. Perhaps I just don't know how to do it as effectively as Curley, who apparently read *Hamlet* with an eye toward using it to show off.

I have before me a newspaper clipping from the *Boston Post,* December 1903. The headline says that the two Curleys "Control One of Boston's Strongest Political Ward Organizations." This is after his conviction for fraud, and well before James Michael Curley became mayor, governor, congressman, political legend. "Never before . . . has the Bay State witnessed the spectacle of such personal power." The *Post* reporter—and undoubtedly many others—wondered how the Curleys had done it.

Curley reading at home. (Courtesy Boston Public Library)

Since then, too, countless opponents have wondered the same thing.

I think, if I understand Curley correctly, that he was not so much interested in the power as he was in what the power enabled him to accomplish. Because men have an innate desire to amass power, the framers of our government created various checks on individuals seeking it. But this is another story—and during Curley's life his political opponents came up with many new ways to check his personal power (forbidding the mayor to succeed himself, limiting the mayor's power to control the city budget, breaking down the link between individual constituents and district representatives) that in the long run hurt the city as a political entity.

One more anecdote about Curley in jail. John Pettingell, the city's superintendent of institutions, happened to visit the Charles Street Jail in 1903 while Curley was an inmate. Pettingell asked about the books on Curley's bedside table, and he learned that the young inmate was reading a biography of Thomas Jefferson. When Pettingell returned to City Hall, he told a young female social worker that James Michael Curley was "one of the most interesting persons I've seen in all my years of service—a fine, good-looking young man." Pettingell had spent half an hour talking with Curley, and he told his young colleague, "You're a young woman, and I'm an old man. Years after I'm dead, you'll be hearing about that man Curley."

2

THE RISE OF
JAMES MICHAEL CURLEY

As a young man James Michael Curley was nervous, unsure of himself, and had little to say. He had always been bright enough—while he was working at Gale's Drug Store in the South End, one customer had offered to pay his way through college in the hopes that young James Michael Curley could become a preacher. The catch was that his would-be patroness was a Protestant, and she expected our young hero to convert. He declined her offer.

He did well at the Dearborn School in Roxbury, though he worked every morning for an hour and a half at the drugstore, ran to school, came back to work during the school's lunch break, and worked every night from four to eleven. He worked all day on Saturdays and Sundays—all day meaning from seven in the morning until eleven at night on Saturday, eight until eleven on Sundays. This job paid him $2.50 a week, enough to pay the family's monthly rent of ten dollars. When he graduated from Dearborn at the age of sixteen, he had missed only three days of work at Gale's.

Jim Curley and his older brother, John, both had to work. Their mother, Sarah, scrubbed floors on Beacon Hill and in the Back Bay; their father, Michael Curley, had died in 1884, when Jim was ten. Emigrating separately from Galway, both Michael and Sarah had arrived in Boston in 1864. Michael was fourteen, Sarah twelve. They married in 1870, had their first son, John, in

1872, and James in 1874; Michael, born in 1879, died two and a half years later.

Michael Curley died on the job. A big man, he boasted that he could lift anything. A foreman bet him he could not lift a four-hundred-pound curbstone. Michael won the bet, but it killed him. He lifted the curb from the wagon and died. Sarah and her children were alone in a world with no social welfare system, no public aid for widows and children.

Curley's extraordinary work ethic was born in these years of struggle. He had a string of jobs—he delivered groceries, sold insurance or bakery supplies, and for nine months worked at the New England Piano Company, where he lost fifty pounds and learned something of the exploitation of labor. Initially paid $7.50 per week, he had been put on piecework; when through his efficiency and industriousness his pay doubled, the management put him back on salary. He knew it was his last day on the job when he spied the top-hatted plant manager striding briskly across the sidewalk outside. Jim picked up a cake of industrial soap used to lubricate the piano strings and threw it out the window, knocking the boss's silk hat off his head.

Storming into the workroom, the enraged manager demanded, "Who threw that soap?" No one spoke.

"I'll give twenty-five dollars [more than three weeks' pay] to the man who'll tell me who threw that soap."

"Make it fifty, and I'll tell you who."

No orator, Curley had ready answers. He went back to delivering groceries. He was spending a few idle minutes in the neighborhood cigar store on Northampton Street one day when the owner, One-Arm Pete Whalen, suggested that Jim run for Common Council. Each ward elected three representatives to this council, which met every Monday. The position paid nothing, but it provided a good place to watch for openings on the city payroll and ways to bring benefits to the neighborhood.

Curley had two problems. First, he had no money. Second, he was not part of the regular organization. Whalen solved the first problem, reaching into his pocket and pulling out ten dollars. The other men in the store pitched in fifteen more, and with that twenty-five dollars Curley went over to Keezer's, the venerable second-hand clothing store in Cambridge, to buy a cutaway coat and striped trousers.

A candidate now must spend huge amounts of money for media "buys," as they are called. Not to do so is political suicide. The media today may exercise control over the political process; in 1897, when Curley first ran, there was entrenched power of a different sort, the ward organization. The ward organization decided who would run for office, and through these elected officials kept a close watch for available city jobs to dispense to voters. Curley's father had obtained his laboring job through Roxbury's ward boss, "Pea Jacket" Maguire. Maguire had given the job to Michael Curley but had later done little for his widow or children. Maguire's organization paid scant attention to the needs of Northampton Street, which is why One-Arm Pete wanted young James Michael to take them on.

One-Arm Pete saw something in James Michael Curley that made him think the young man could win. In his spare time from work at the drugstore, piano factory, and grocer's, Curley was a tireless community volunteer. He organized dances and social events for the Ancient Order of Hibernians, and he spent hundreds of hours every year planning Roxbury's St. Patrick's Day Parade. If you have organized a dance or a parade, you know how tedious the work can be—but Jim Curley seemed to thrive on this kind of organizational detail. Curley involved himself with other parades and social activities—planning, raising money, doing the behind-the-scenes work that ensures an event will go smoothly.

He and his brother John taught Sunday School at St. Patrick's Church on Northampton Street, where Jim organized dances, reunions, and festivals. Attendance at these social events and at Sunday Mass swelled. The church could comfortably seat four hundred, but crowds at Mass overflowed into the street outside, and parishioners even waited in front of the fire station across Northampton Street to form the Communion line. Curley strug-

Young James Michael Curley. (Courtesy Boston Public Library)

gled through the crowded church to take up the collection. He did not stop at the church door, but, collection basket in hand, went out onto the steps, on the sidewalk, and even across the street. Seeing that St. Patrick's could not accommodate all who wanted to attend, Curley led the way in raising money to build St. Philip's Church, just a few hundred yards away. St. Philip's opened in 1899.

When Pea Jacket Maguire died in 1896, control of his organization passed to his lieutenants, John Dever and Charles Quirk. Quirk and Dever had inherited a functioning political organization; they did not need to build it through personal loyalty and political favors. Mundane tasks—helping an immigrant get through the line at immigration, helping another fill out a job application, preventing a family from being evicted—were time consuming, and they no longer offered the kind of return the organization needed. Dever and Quirk no longer had the patience for this kind of activity.

Curley did. He was never too busy to help someone who needed it. Vote by vote, he had been building his own organization. People in the ward knew him through his work at St. Patrick's, through the Ancient Order of Hibernians, or through his attention to their mundane problems. Dever and Quirk became unapproachable. No local officeholder can afford that—nearly anything else, but never, never unapproachable. Curley was never unapproachable.

Dever and Quirk barred Curley from speaking at their campaign events, so he set out to talk to every voter in the ward, knocking on their doors, a most approachable candidate.

Here is the activist Curley at work. James T. Kenney was music marshal in the annual Labor Day parade. On the miserable, rainy night before the parade in 1898, Curley rang Kenney's doorbell. Kenney did not know the drenched young man in a rubber coat and rubber boots who had come to call on him.

"What do you want?" Kenney asked.

Curley told him, "I want to put some men to work." Kenney told him he had all the musicians he needed and started to close the door.

Curley asked, "How much do they pay the man who carries the bass drum?" Kenney told him three dollars, for two or three hours of work.

"Mr. Kenney, I've got ten men that money will be a godsend to. Can you put them on?"

Kenney recalled the episode years later. "Did I give those ten men jobs? You can bet your last dollar that I did. And from that day to this I've sworn by James M. Curley. He is and always has been a man of energy, and of ideas, with more of the will to help and make the world a better place to live in than any other ten men." Here he was out on "the dirtiest night you ever saw" so he could help ten men earn a few dollars. It was an errand too small for Dever and Quirk, but not for Curley. He earned the loyalty of eleven men—ten who carried the drums, and James Kenney.

It would be pleasant to report that Curley beat the machine and was elected to the Common Council; but it would not be true. After the ballots were cast, the ward committee counted the votes, and though Curley estimated that he won by three hundred votes, the ward committee declared him down by two hundred.

Curley ran again the next year, with the same strategy—talk to every voter. The city had recently barred campaigning outside polling places. It is something of a Boston custom to make voters run a gauntlet on their way to cast ballots on Election Day. Curley and his rivals stood outside the polls, silently watching the voters walk in. But when groups of recent Irish immigrants entered, Curley would say, in Gaelic, "Don't forget the boy from home!"

Again he was declared a loser. He was getting closer—he estimated that he won by five hundred votes, the ward committee declared him the loser by one hundred votes. After another year of doing the kinds of public services that Dever and Quirk were too big for, he said, "In 1899 I won by a thousand votes—and they didn't dare to count me out."

As one of seventy-five councilors, Curley had little real power. He studied parliamentary procedure, and he proposed that Saturdays be a half day for city workers, pushed to install sanitary plumbing in the city's public schools, and pressed for enforcement of the eight-hour workday.

More important, he helped his constituents. They trooped to the family apartment on Harrison Avenue, where Sarah Curley reported on who had visited and what their problems were. James announced that he would be home on Wednesday and Friday evenings to receive visitors. Anyone with a problem knew he or she could talk to Jim Curley.

Every Wednesday and every Friday, between twenty-five and fifty people would come to call. Curley saw that they fell into three categories. First were the people with financial problems—

unable to buy food or coal, unable to pay the doctor's bill or the rent. Second were those in legal trouble—those whose children had been charged with vagrancy or truancy, people facing eviction. Finally, there were the unemployed. For the first, Curley would ask questions, take careful notes, and write letters to doctors, fuel suppliers, grocers, or, if he had cash, make a small gift. For those in legal trouble, Curley would go to the courthouse or police station. He would have nothing to do with either drunks or "wife-beaters." The former were unreliable, the latter reprehensible. Curley would meet the jobless at City Hall, and set out to help them find work.

Roxbury at this time of corporate mergers and economic restructuring was shedding its industrial base. When the Pearson Cordage Company plant was shut down, twelve hundred jobs left Roxbury; the New England Piano Company shut down in 1902 and another twelve hundred men lost jobs; the Putnam Nail Company closed in 1903, throwing three hundred men out of work; the Howard Watch Company shed 20 percent of its workforce; the Chadwick Lead Works and the Guyer Hat Company reduced their labor forces. Finding jobs for the unemployed was Curley's priority for most of his public life.

"We have tramped Atlantic Avenue and the waterfront appealing for work," he said in 1903. "Men who made pianos have become longshoremen. Watchmakers have taken to driving trucks. So it goes on. We assisted in securing employment in New Hampshire for fifty men."

Over the first decade of his political career, Curley claimed that in an average year he prevented twenty-five people, particularly juveniles, from getting criminal records; forestalled seven evictions or repossessions of furniture; and found five hundred jobs for unemployed men and women. From my own experience, I know that finding jobs for people is not a rewarding use of time—the line only gets longer and there is inevitable disappointment. For Curley, this was an essential part of his public life.

He was not addressing what social scientists or political theorists might consider the root causes of these problems. He was not proposing tax incentives to keep factories operating in Roxbury, or encouraging banks to invest in his community. He was dealing with problems at the human level, microscopically. Often the human problem he encountered led him to propose a public initiative—when he found, for example, that he was spending time dealing with juvenile delinquency, he tried to find a way to get young people off the streets. But he found, as have others, that many of these solutions are less effective than direct involvement with a person's life.

Other ward leaders did similar things, but sometimes with expectations that were at least morally questionable. If the ward leader found you a job, you were expected to contribute to his campaign account. But Curley did all this with no such demands or expectations. He earned something far more precious than campaign contributions—he earned the person's loyalty and gratitude. This loyalty and gratitude were in themselves worth far more politically outside the ward than were jobs secured inside it. If a candidate for mayor, for Congress, or for state legislature knew that Curley controlled the vote of Ward 17, Curley would be of inestimable political value.

Curley never lost this capacity to help others. When he became mayor and moved his family to a home on the Jamaicaway, visitors would call every morning with their problems and requests. Curley—as a congressman, as mayor—never turned anyone away. The *Boston Post* in 1911 summed up the difference between James Michael Curley and the other Boston ward leaders. "If Martin Lomasney," the leader of the West End (a neighborhood that no longer exists), "were given a million dollars tomorrow he would put it into real estate. Mayor Fitzgerald would use it as an anchor to windward against the coming of a stormy political day. Smiling James Donovan would gather a chosen band of good friends about him and give them the 'good time' of their lives. Curley would hand it out in bunches to every constituent who came along with a hard luck story, on the theory that 'there's lots more millions where that one came from.'"

Today millions of dollars are spent to persuade voters to favor a candidate. The money distances and insulates candidates from the very constituency they strive to win over. Direct person-to-person involvement becomes rare. The candidate is a product. He is sold to a public to whom he is unknown. Indeed, the less well known the candidate is the better for the candidate. His defects are hidden; they become known over the course of his term of office. And he will continue to keep his distance. Familiarity assures contempt.

Old-timers around the State House told me that when Curley was governor, people would wait for him in the Archway on Mount Vernon Street—this was during the Depression—to ask him for a few bucks. Curley would always reach into his pocket. Today, can anyone get close to a governor? Approach a governor in our times and you risk trouble with the law. This is what inspired that tremendous loyalty I saw among the senior citizens gathered at the Brunswick Hotel to cheer him on at the end of his public life. They were not memorializing public policy or political philosophy, but thanking a person who had been their mayor, their governor, their friend.

3

CURLEY CAMPAIGNING

My wife, Mary, and I were in Ireland, and Irish television was broadcasting a show about Boston. Naturally, it featured a segment on Boston politics, and the subject turned to James Michael Curley. What a surprise to hear a familiar voice booming forth, "I, James Michael Curley, will take the useless Gold Dome from the top of the State House, and turn it upside down, and place it in the middle of Andrew Square in South Boston and let the little children use it as a swimming pool. Curley makes no rash promises! So when you go to the polls on Tuesday next—vote early, vote often, vote Curley!"

The cadenced, mellifluous tones were unmistakable. But neither the words nor the voice was Curley's—they were mine! It was my own voice, my imitation of Curley, which I had done countless times throughout the city. All of us aspiring young Irish American politicians had "done" Curley, not as an act—none of us said, "Here's my James Michael Curley impression"—but had picked up the habit over the years of lapsing into the voice and manner of the master. Curley was such a part of Boston's lore and legend that all of us sought to be like him in superficial ways. We tried to learn what made him so magical. It may have been an effort to tap into the magic. You could not have an event without one or all of us "doing" Curley. Mike Ward, known as "The Professor," would be speaking and suddenly lapse into Curley. John Cremins would come to the St. Patrick's Day Breakfast, dressed in the full regalia of the Ancient and Honorable Artillery Company, and in the course of his remarks his voice would become Curley's.

The Curley legend—how much of the legend is true, and how much truth can we discern beneath it? Even my own imitation—the overblown rhetoric, the exaggerated promise of turning the State House dome into a swimming pool, followed by the outlandish statement "Curley makes no rash promises!" became accepted, at least to the Irish viewers, as good entertainment. Not only to the Irish—passing through the halls of the Massachusetts State House, I have overheard one of the Doric Dames, our volunteer docents, telling a group of visitors that "Governor Curley once promised to turn the dome into a swimming pool in South Boston!"

Curley was a spellbinding orator. I remember when it must have been 1952, and Eisenhower was running for president. Eisenhower made some remark praising Oliver Cromwell—the leader of the English Civil War of the 1640s and 1650s. Surely Ike did not realize how viciously Cromwell had treated the Irish, but Curley was quick to remind him. I remember hearing Curley deliver his radio address: "Tonight my subject will be two generals—Cromwell and Eisenhower."

Some of it now sounds like pure bombast, and you wonder how he got away with it. J. R. Milne did a series on Curley that appeared in the *Boston Post* in 1930. Milne concluded this life history of Curley, just elected mayor for the third time, with this amazing anecdote. He had asked the mayor to recall the birth of his first son. "It may be," Curley mused, "that I am different from many men." He certainly believed that. He went on to say that marriage and birth were both "holy sacraments," and that when his wife was about to give birth, Curley never left the house. "When they wanted to find me, they always knew where I might be found. I would be outside her door, kneeling down, and saying the rosary."

Would anyone believe this? It strains my capacity to believe, and yet, according to Milne, when he told people "what James Michael Curley had told me, I saw tears in one woman's eyes."

The Curley family, about 1921. Left to right: *Leo, Paul, Mary, the baby George, daughter Mary, Mayor Curley, James M. Curley Jr., and Dorothea. (Courtesy Boston Public Library)*

Curley could get away with this because he had developed a personal connection with his audience, but also because he was marvelously entertaining. He trained his voice; he put on a show. I remember seeing him speaking at Columbus Park (now Joe Moakley Park), standing to the rear of his car, with the green neon sign—CURLEY—across the back window. There was excitement. Candidates for the various offices had followed him to the park, where they too would have an audience. It was a full-fledged rally as Curley lambasted his opponents and promised great things. The people of South Boston would prove loyal once again as he enumerated the benefits of his administration: the health unit on Dorchester Street, the L Street Bathhouse on Columbia Road, and a beach that would rival Waikiki. Julius Ansel of old Ward 14 in Dorchester was among the host of Curleycrats showing their enthusiasm for their candidate. In later years Ansel became a legislative colleague of mine. At the end he ran against John Collins. Ansel had Curley's boldness. One day I met him on School Street, and with a microphone in hand he was facing the Old City Hall, shouting, "Mr. Mayor, clean out your desk!"

Once Curley had bested the Dever-Quirk combination in 1899, he had two choices: either join forces with the machine, or eliminate it. Curley was not about to join the organization. He would become the organization. Dever and Quirk held forth at the Jackson Club, which met at the Vine Street Church on Dudley Street, a former church building converted into the ward committee office. (In his second term as mayor, Curley replaced his old rivals' headquarters with a municipal building.) Curley tried to become chair of the ward committee in 1900; he failed, but the next year he and eight others walked out of the Jackson Club to form the Tammany Club, modeled on the New York organization of that name. Renting the former Temperance Society headquarters above a Hampden Street bakery, Curley opened the Tammany Club in time for July 4, 1902.

Here, with his weekly talks on every conceivable subject, Curley developed his unique speaking ability, experimenting with his voice and taking lessons to improve it. He stood with his shoulders back, his stomach and chest protruding, his hands at his sides. For variety, he would invite other speakers to entertain his audience. One week he brought in a Harvard professor to speak against Irish independence. The professor barely missed being knocked out by a cuspidor.

These were tough audiences. Curley's opponent in 1905, Mike Drew, pledged to resign from the Board of Aldermen if Curley, an ex-convict, was also elected. "I will not take my seat . . . on the ground of common decency. No decent man would sit with him in the aldermanic chamber." Though born in Ireland, Drew had served in the English army. On the outskirts of a Ward 17 rally, Curley spied Drew's wagon, carrying anti-Curley signs. "This hireling of England," Curley said, pointing to the Drew wagon, "says he is going to beat James M. Curley! What have the men of Ward 17 to say to this British Hessian?"

The men of Ward 17 attacked the wagon, which narrowly escaped on three wheels, making its way to Newspaper Row, on Washington Street. (Years later, Curley appointed Drew to the city collector's office.)

Another opponent had one good speech, but he could not speak extemporaneously. The speech was new to each new crowd, but Curley needed to hear it only once or twice to know it by heart. In his peroration the candidate demanded, "Where is this coward Curley? Let this coward Curley stand up before me, and answer what I have to say!" There would be an emphatic silence.

One night Curley slipped into the Vine Street Church with his coat over his head. When the candidate demanded, "Where is this coward Curley? Let this coward Curley stand up before me, and answer what I have to say!" the "coward Curley" popped his head out of his coat and said, "Here I am, Tom!"

His opponent sputtered; the audience laughed.

The 1909 mayoral race, between John Fitzgerald and James J. Storrow, was one of the classic battles in Boston politics. Fitzgerald had been elected to one term as mayor in 1905—the first ward boss and the first son of immigrant parents to be elected mayor. (Hugh O'Brien, himself an Irish immigrant, had been mayor in the 1880s, and Patrick Collins, another Irish immigrant, had been elected mayor in 1901 and 1903.) The Brahmin establishment saw the handwriting on the wall with Fitzgerald's elevation. They hoped to eliminate this kind of ward bossism or Irish power, so they proposed to reform the city government—a weaker city council, comprising only nine members chosen at large, and a stronger mayor to serve a four-year (rather than two-year) term.

The campaign was stormy and violent. The more enlightened citizens found it shocking that Storrow's speeches in the ethnic wards were interrupted by boos and catcalls. It seemed the campaign would reach its nadir when Storrow came to address Ward 17 at the Vine Street Church. Tom Curley could barely be heard as he introduced his candidate, Storrow; the crowd called Tom

Curley a traitor and offered to scalp him. Storrow must have feared for his own life as he prepared to address this angry mob of Jim Curley's henchmen. Jim Curley's allies were always "henchmen," while the good candidate's allies were progressives, or reformers, or citizens, or, more recently, "resource people," according to the objective observers in the press. But when Storrow began to speak, the crowd grew quiet. Very quiet. With no emotion, no expression, no acknowledgment that Storrow was speaking, Jim Curley's crowd let him read his prepared text to the very end. And when he finished, there would be no applause, no questions, no acknowledgment that he had just presented his case for being mayor.

This was much more devastating than a tossed cuspidor.

I remember, nearly fifty years after this episode, seeing Curley speaking in Flood Square in South Boston, castigating Mayor John B. Hynes, the "little clerk" who defeated him in 1949 and again in 1951. Followers of all other candidates turned out to see Curley, because he was so entertaining, and rival candidates came because Curley drew the crowds. This was risky because Curley still could spy an opportunity. Curley had demolished more hecklers than most of us hear in a lifetime. Curley remarked, after his denunciation of Hynes and the "New Boston," "Of course, everything you have heard me say about Mayor Hynes goes twice for John Powers, right down there at the end of M Street." The crowd turned toward M Street, imagining John Powers crouching there.

Curley made his campaign attacks very personal. A perceptive account of Curley appeared in the midst of the 1921 campaign for mayor. "Watch him in this campaign," the reporter, John Bantry, wrote. "The Boston Elevated 10-cent fare is a sore spot with the public. Will Curley attack that musty old corporation? No. He will heap scorn on the head of Robert Winsor and charge him with being personally responsible if the motorman fails to see you at the white post.

"The public demands a human sacrifice," and Curley would deliver it.

This campaign profile (the *Post* profiled each of the candidates in 1921) went on to say that Curley "deliberately cheapens himself in a campaign," that he "appeals to the mob by saying the things he knows will win their applause and stir their passions. He loses his dignity and his regard for the exact truth." Bantry remarked that in this way Curley was no worse than many of his rivals, except for the fact that Curley "knows better and most of the others don't." The most extraordinary thing about this profile is that Curley distributed it as a campaign pamphlet.

Curley came up in a rough time, when public speakers were lucky to escape with their lives. There was a time in 1908 or 1909 when Curley came to speak to a crowd, and someone yelled, "There's Curley, the desperado!" Curley did not see the heckler, but he did see another local politico, Tom Joyce, shaking his fist at Curley.

"Ah, I see my old friend Tom Joyce, the King of the Crapshooters," Curley said. Joyce shook his fist at Curley, who went on: "See his gestures? Can't you read them? 'The baby wants it! Come seven!' That's what his gestures mean." Then Curley turned on "Smiling Jim" Donovan of Ward 9 and Jim Doyle of Ward 12: "Jim Donovan, the smiling Jinker, the King Dodo of Ward 9, is against me. He has put his puppet, Jim Doyle, the Prince Popo of Ward 12, into the fight against our Jerry Good." From then on, Donovan and Doyle were "King Dodo and Prince Popo." City Councilor Kitty Craven in later years would deliver similar bombast against her foes in Ward 18, Hyde Park: she called her opponents Charlie Patrone, Herb Cantwell, and Michael Paul Feeney "Kukla, Fran, and Ollie," a reference to a trio of puppets.

Curley mocked Donovan's extravagant wardrobe. "We are not afraid of Donovan's money, or Donovan's 250 suits, or 250 pairs of shoes, or 200 pairs of checkered pants." Curley turned Donovan's elegant dressing into an attack on presumed wealth, though Curley later told a reporter, "Of course he didn't have the outfit I accused him of having, but he always managed to look pretty well." Curley could not resist this line of ridicule, and he embellished freely.

One night he told a crowd about meeting Smiling Jim Donovan's valet, who could barely lift his right arm. The poor valet, Curley said, had to press Donovan's 250 suits every week. "'One man can't do that alone—not and shine 250 pairs of shoes, too. So I've been telling Mr. Donovan—either he gets an extra valet to spell me, or I quit my job.'"

Curley asked those in the crowd if they knew where Donovan was at that moment. "He's down at the Hotel Woodcock," Curley told them, "and he's eating a big, succulent five-dollar steak with mushrooms [pausing a moment to let this fact sink in], and he's got a bottle of burgundy at his elbow. What do you think of that? Did you men ever eat a big, succulent, five-dollar steak and wash it down with a bottle of burgundy?"

"No!" the crowd yelled.

"Do you want to?"

Curley said that their resounding "Yes" could be heard for eighteen blocks.

"Well," Curley said, "if Jim Donovan's your friend, he'd surely want to invite you to eat a steak and drink a bottle of burgundy with him. I'll tell you his address and you can go put the matter up with him."

Former Congressman William McNary of South Boston maneuvered Curley into the congressional race of 1910. McNary wanted Curley in the race to draw away the Roxbury vote from the incumbent, Joseph O'Connell of Dorchester. McNary assured Curley his only interest was in beating O'Connell, but once Curley was in, McNary jumped in, too. Before Curley thought to do it, McNary and O'Connell bought up all the billboards in the district. O'Connell advertised himself as "Able, Active, and Aggressive." McNary's signs said: "Send a Big Man to Do a Big Job." Curley pasted his own streamers onto the McNary and O'Connell billboards: "Elect a Humble Man: James Michael Curley."

Curley vowed not to attack his opponents. "There will be no more harsh sayings from me. I will turn the soft answer on my rivals' wrath. I shall speak no ill of them." He quoted Shake-speare:

> *Kind words are more than coronets,*
> *And simple faith than Norman blood.*

He would find more imaginative ways to best his adversaries. McNary and O'Connell began to mock "Humble Jimmie," and Humble Jimmie responded with a card quoting Robert Burns:

> *Oh, wid some power the giftie gie us*
> *To see ourselves as others see us!*
> *It wod frae monie a blunder free us*
> *An foolish notion!*

Beneath this he placed McNary's slogan, "A Big Man, A Big Place," and O'Connell's "Able, Active, and Aggressive."

Some observers said that Curley's literary allusions were "as good as the Harvard course in literature, only much more diverting."

Seeing Curley was making friends throughout the district, McNary attacked his personal honesty. Curley, after all, had been in jail six years earlier. McNary spoke of his own personal integrity, contrasting himself with Curley. Curley sent a man calling himself Diogenes, clad in toga and a laurel wreath, carrying a lamp through the streets of South Boston and calling out that he was looking for "the honest man—McNary."

McNary had the man arrested and blasted Curley for the cheap political stunt. But the next day, when Diogenes was brought before the South Boston Municipal Court, Curley defended him. Why, he demanded, was Diogenes arrested? Had he committed a crime by "calling McNary an honest man?"

Case dismissed. Curley elected. But two terms in Congress were enough, and in 1913 he set his sights on the job he really wanted, mayor of Boston. This time, after he forced John Fitzger-ald out of the race, his opponent was the competent but colorless

Thomas Kenny of South Boston, president of the City Council. All the political leaders supported Kenny—Curley called him a "fine, clean man," and the Democratic City Committee endorsed Kenny unanimously. Curley called the City Committee "empty egg-shells" and set out to win the election, announcing, "My velour is in the center of the circle [it would not be enough for Curley merely to throw his hat into the ring], there to remain until my opponent succeeds in accomplishing the impossible mathematical proposition of squaring that circle January 13, 1914."

Curley toured the city with his Tammany entourage. In South Boston singers and musicians drew the crowds, then entertained them before Curley's arrival. Curley came to Flood Square, packed with disgruntled Fitzgerald supporters and Kenny backers. Curley announced he would carry Kenny's home precinct, and he decreed, "If he lived in a five-family house, I'd get four of the five votes."

As Curley spoke, Fitzgerald supporters filtered through the crowd to disrupt the rally with calculated heckling. Curley taunted, "You're nothing but a pack of second-story workers, milk-bottle robbers, and doormat thieves [pickpockets]. I'll be elected mayor of Boston, and you don't like it. Here I am. Do any of you bums want to step up here and make anything of it?" The thugs had been waiting for a chance to disrupt Curley, but he mesmerized them. The hecklers no doubt had heard of Curley inviting a heckler to join him on the platform, and then knocking him out with a surprise punch. None of the "second-story workers, milk-bottle robbers, or doormat thieves" came forward to share his platform in Flood Square, and none heckled him.

Curley was most effective when he used his withering sarcasm and his carefully cadenced voice to ridicule a heckler or an opponent. (The hecklers were usually agents of the opponent.) Throughout the campaign for mayor Kenny spoke of tax rates, loan amortization, and very specific details of the budgetary process. It was not the stuff of great political theater or oratory. As Kenny traveled through the city putting audiences to sleep, Curley barnstormed with his brass band, his singers, and his main event, himself. Curley promised more playgrounds, better schools, sandy beaches, public gymnasiums, improved streets and highways. Kenny asked how the city would pay for all these things and went back to discussing the cost of borrowing money. Kenny began to see, even in the absence of public opinion polls, that the issue was not the tax rate, but a better city, and that people really seemed to like Curley. So if Curley was the issue, Kenny would go on the attack. He criticized Curley as a "charlatan, a vendor of magic municipal remedies, a pretender." Kenny even brought up the old charge: "Where was Curley during the Spanish American War?" Curley had earlier explained that he was kept out of the war by hemorrhoids. It was an interesting response; the Democratic Party had been ambivalent about the war, seeing it as the beginning of an American empire, and an end to the republic. Curley dodged the whole issue.

Kenny had already established himself as a dull speaker; Curley took advantage of this. At his own campaign events, Curley read Kenny's speech—verbatim, but with his own particular inflections, including Kenny's withering attack on himself as "a charlatan, a vendor of magic municipal remedies, a pretender. Where was Curley during the Spanish American War?" Curley would then pause for dramatic effect, look at his audience, and raise his index finger. "Naughty, naughty, Tommy!"

Curley understood that the spoken word—particularly the word spoken by such practiced instruments as his vocal cords—must have a certain elevation beyond the straightforward text of the printed page. This was before the era of sound-bites, the thirty-second television or radio ad. Curley was working in a different medium—when radio came on the scene, he changed his delivery a bit to master this new medium; had he been around a bit later, he would have mastered television as well. Curley accepted the world as he found it. In his day the campaign ethic was to deliver a series of speeches at rallies across the city, the state, or the country if one wanted to hold office; the political system itself was based on the wards of the city, the neighborhoods, and the various ward leaders held sway. Curley did not set out to change this; he sought to master it. Were he seeking office today, he would try to master the political system of today and not lament that it was not more conducive to the attainment of his own ambitious ends.

Curley wound up the 1913 campaign with a tour throughout the city, and he alighted from his open car to address a crowd gathered in front of St. Augustine's Church in South Boston. "Here in the shadow of the spires of St. Augustine's," he said to the crowd, "I am reminded by Brother Kenny of those beautiful words in that beautiful prayer, 'Our Father, who art in heaven, hallowed be thy name.'" As he led the crowd in the Lord's Prayer, Curley spied a man getting too close to his car. "'Give us this day our daily bread.'" Now the man was lifting Curley's fur coat from the backseat. "'And forgive us our trespasses.'" Turning to his body-guard, Curley said beneath his breath, "Get that son of a bitch heisting my fur coat from my car"; he then turned back to the crowd, "'As we forgive those who trespass against us. Lead us not into temptation, but deliver us from evil. Amen.'"

It is difficult, if not impossible, to convey on the printed page Curley's effectiveness as a speaker, just as it is impossible to convey his sharp wit. Indeed, his wit was biting—one journalist wrote that Curley lacked a real sense of humor, that "Curley's idea of a joke is always touched with irony and the sarcastic." Curley's "humorous allusions to his opponents" were always "barbed with biting sarcasm." Though Curley might not intend it, "his wit is savage and unkind." And very funny, unless you happened to be the object of it.

In the case of most of the stories passed down by those who heard them, you did have to be there to catch the humor. His humor—like most political humor—came out of particular circumstances, and what seemed vitally important on one day was forgotten by the end of the week. Curley did get off many hilarious (at least to those not targeted) one-liners, which taken out of context might as well be fragments of cuneiform.

Here is a speech Congressman Curley gave to the members of the City Council in 1912. Curley knew that his host, Mayor

Fitzgerald, expected to run for reelection. Curley's brief remarks played on his own ambition.

"I am a candidate for mayor in 1914." We can picture the diners listening intently after Curley lobbed that bombshell. "I shall run on a platform drawn up by the Finance Commission and approved by Laurence Minot." The Finance Commission was a state agency set up by the Republican legislature to oversee the Democrats in Boston. "I would like to announce, in this connection also, that Robert J. Bottomley of the Good Government Association is to be my campaign manager." The Good Government Association was another Yankee Republican institution intent on civic reform; its members typically were referred to as the "Goo-Goos."

We can picture Fitzgerald and the councilors falling out of their chairs at this; we can also picture some poor sarcastically challenged historian stumbling on the speech and concluding that in 1912 Curley was approved by the Finance Commission and the Good Government Association.

Then there are the throwaway lines: at a function at the Tammany Club, a valiant piano player entertained with great enthusiasm but little skill. Curley had to interrupt to make an announcement, and when he was done he said, "The village blacksmith will now resume." One of the stalwarts of Curley's Tammany Club was a loquacious fellow named McMonogogue, whom Curley always introduced as McMonologue. A candidate for Congress told a crowd he hoped his wife "would be the wife of a congressman," and Curley rose and said, "Then why don't you drop dead and let her marry one," as he took over the microphone.

Curley was a magnetic and charismatic speaker, able to connect with an audience, but he was a political loner—not maintaining any real political friendships, though thousands of Boston voters felt a personal bond with him. In many ways the public persona of Curley—the rascal king, the man of the people—belies the real person. His whole life was a public one, and virtually every Bostonian who recalls Curley has some story about

Mayor Curley, with his wife Mary at his side, throws out the first pitch at Fenway Park. The Boston baseball teams, the Braves and the Red Sox, won three World Championships in Curley's first term. (Courtesy Boston Public Library)

Curley touching his or her life in a personal way. But few ever knew the "real" Curley. He was an intensely private man, guarding his own and his family's privacy zealously.

Curley had few real friends. During the 1921 campaign, John Bantry of the *Boston Post* profiled Curley, and he noted, "He seeks no man's personal friendship, much as he would like his political friendship." Curley's first wife, Mary, who married him in 1906, was in many ways his closest counselor. Mary Curley died after a long illness in 1930; seven of their nine children died before their father.

Standish Wilcox, a brilliant newspaperman, attached himself to Curley during his first congressional fight. Wilcox died soon after Curley returned from an Italian jaunt in 1931. Curley had bitter fallings-out with most of his political allies. Tom Curley, his first political partner, with whom he had created the Tammany Club back in 1902, was by the end of that decade one of his inveterate enemies.

"I loved Jim Curley like a brother," Tom Curley recalled after he had been ousted from the Tammany Club in 1908. "And I stood more from him than I would from any man living. I despise him now as much as I loved him. I have found him out. He will promise anything and perform nothing. In his five years in the Board of Aldermen he has done nothing for the ward. He has even prevented the ward from getting the playground which it needs so badly. That's why I quit him. I could not stand such an imposition upon the ward. I have him beaten to a frazzle now and he knows it."

Tom Curley was wrong about a number of things, first that he had beaten Curley to a frazzle, and, perhaps as significant, that Curley opposed the playground. What politician in his right mind would try to block the city from putting a playground in his own ward? James Michael Curley did. Why? Because Curley actually wanted the playground built. The other aldermen were either Republicans or Curley foes. Curley knew they would turn down anything he proposed. In order to get the playground, Curley vocally opposed it, allowing his opponents on the Board of Aldermen to force the playground onto Curley's ward. The deception was so complete that even Tom Curley was fooled, which suggests that of the two Curleys he was not the sharper.

4
CURLEY IN POWER

"When Congressman Curley is in Boston," one of the papers wrote in 1913, "though his political influence is now supposed to be with the federal department heads, he is just as busy pulling favors at City Hall as when he was an alderman and councilor. Members of the present City Council are rarely seen in the building but for favors or other things until a meeting day, but Curley is always racing from one office to another for his constituents. Those who know the Congressman well say that this is the secret of his success in politics so far—that he is always 'on the job' for his constituent."

Curley always was "on the job" for his constituents. There is a hope that whoever it is we elect will do the job for which he's elected. There was the reassuring sense that while Curley was the mayor, Curley was in truth the mayor—for better or for worse. It was reassuring that the major decisions were not being made by a banker or a newspaper publisher or a ward boss. It was the judgment of Curley, the man elected to do the job, that was being brought to bear on the city's business. It is a betrayal of the electorate for any elected official to sacrifice his judgment to the desires and interests of publishers and businessmen who have not been elected. In all likelihood press people and business people, if they had the courage to put their names on a ballot, would be rejected.

If someone had a problem, he or she did not need to "know someone" who would speak to the mayor. A man could speak to

Curley at work. (Courtesy Boston Public Library)

the mayor himself. In his first term as mayor, Curley claimed to have talked to as many people as were registered to vote in the city. When Curley made grandiose claims about seeing two hundred people every day, fifty thousand per year, we can be sure of one thing: he was shamelessly employing hyperbole. He could not have been telling the truth. Do the math. Count the minutes and the hours. If Curley did talk to two hundred people every day, when did he do anything else?

I am reminded of Representative Jim Craven of Jamaica Plain, who expressed envy that "you South Boston politicians can march along, greeting your constituents by the tens of thousands, while not one of them can get your ear. It may seem like personal campaigning, but you might as well be on CNN for all the access these folks have." In truth this parade participation is much fun, and it provides a chance to say hello. On the other hand, John Kerrigan, a longtime South Boston city councilor, believed that the more banquets he attended as an incumbent, the more votes he lost, as requests for impossible favors resulted in disappoint-ments for supplicants.

Once one becomes an officeholder, such things as knocking on doors for votes become impractical. People have many problems. Many will ask for the most impossible things. They are dis-pleased to be told that their request is beyond the politician's ability to grant. It is a melancholy reality for incumbents that the challenger, having no office, is free to raise false hopes in the hearts of the constituents. I remember that at that Brunswick

Meeting the people: Curley and his son James Jr. in a parade. (Courtesy Boston Public Library)

Hotel party on Primary Day in 1951, a sweet little woman told me that she had asked Curley for a job. "Come see me in January when I'm the mayor!" With this assurance she had devoted herself to the campaign. Let's suppose that Curley was elected, and could hire 111 people—would he stop saying this when he met the 112th person? Curley could make promises; for most of his career he was able to deliver on them. But the claim that Curley spoke with every voter in the district must have been as much an exaggeration as the promise that he would find work for every deserving constituent.

The point of all these stories of accessibility is not that he was completely accessible. The point is that an ordinary citizen had as much access as the president of State Street Bank, and that ultimately it would be Curley's judgment, not the counsel of an insider, that would be brought to bear on the city's problems. You did not need to go through an intermediary; you could go directly to City Hall. All the city's ward leaders had their power eclipsed during Curley's tenure, except for Martin Lomasney, who had built his power base through the same kind of dedication to constituent services.

Curley learned that one city commissioner did not allow the public to come into his office. He was impossible to see, difficult to get on the phone. The mayor sent word to all heads of city agencies that "coming down to earth a little more in meeting the public is a pretty good idea." Department heads worked for the people of Boston.

This is a salutary policy, and it also makes good political sense. In my office every year I would stand on a chair to address the staff, insisting that anyone with a complaint, whether it was within the purview of our office or not, had to be treated with respect and deserved the courtesy of being listened to.

And no one of us is above that. If someone here believes that only legislative matters are his responsibility, then he should leave now. When you help these people who come through here, you are learning what bedevils such people in their ordinary lives. You are then better prepared to craft legislation and shepherd it through the process. You may even recognize that our intrusive government frequently becomes the source of new problems, no matter how well-intentioned the intrusion into people's lives may be. This direct experience is better than any dry study of the plight of ordinary people. Help them, learn from them, and in doing so, help your legislator to be reelected.

I recall a lawyer who asked that I hire his much-graduated spouse as my aide. "She would work on legislative policy," he said, "but not on constituent services." I informed him directly that everyone in my office, including me, works on constituent matters. Sorry that I cannot help her.

Imagine suggesting to a constituent that we need not bother ourselves with his or her petty concerns. That person will have a story to tell for the next thirty years. I think of my old friend Joe Moakley, sitting out at Castle Island writing down the problems people brought to him there. On the other hand, if all we do is appear in public, listening to people, we will get nothing done.

As long as that is true—that we as ordinary citizens have access to our elected officials, and that our views will have the same gravity with them as the views of the bank presidents or newspaper publishers, then we have a sense of ourselves as being in charge. Curley, by the strength of his personality, reassured his constituents that he was their man in charge, and that he truly represented them. He sensed the tremendous responsibility he owed to the voters who had put their confidence in him. He knew that if he was to maintain the sort of public confidence he had earned, he had to be at it full-time. And indeed that was characteristic of all his days in office. They were full days. There was no absenteeism, no hint of absenteeism, no hint of lack of interest.

He was fulfilling this hope, especially of the people who are in fact ordinary people. This accounts for their loyalty to him. He sensed that this was what they wanted of him, and by God, this was what they would have. Office seekers noted his appeal and sought to emulate him. Politics became a very personal matter in that community.

This brand of politics, very personal, very special, gathered its own spirit from Curley. It is no wonder that people who are more sophisticated, more mobile, less connected to the older neighborhoods of the city look on this personal, intense connection with puzzlement. Why, the more sophisticated people will ask, would people be loyal to him? Why would they do this when all of us know it's ridiculous—this is a seriously flawed individual. But the scoffers cannot understand the importance of this critical, fundamental reality, that Curley's people saw his election as their way of determining their own fate through this office. Through him, they were able to keep their own influence. They could have a genuine influence—a serious and honest influence—on the future of their city, and the more displeasure they witnessed on the part of the bankers, business leaders, and newspaper publishers, then the more certain they were that he was simply not beholden to the powerful. He was their man, and the displeasure and wrath of the powerful was the price that he would pay. The intense disapproval of high-placed Curley foes reassured the electorate of one thing: the leaders of State Street did not like him; therefore he should be elected. Frequently it is those who disapprove of a candidate that informs us of what he is.

By the way, people speak of Boston politics as fascinating, though it is less so now. When it was more pervasive and more intriguing and more entertaining, that was due to the presence of this individual, James Michael Curley, who fulfilled the urge or something stronger of the ordinary people to be masters of their own fate and community.

The fact that Curley dedicated himself so fully allowed him to perform one of the first great acts of his mayoral service. Curley noticed how dirty City Hall had become, its walls coated with smoke and grime, its floors covered with tobacco and dirt. He ordered the place cleaned thoroughly as befit the people's government. On leaving City Hall that first night on the job, he met the cleaning women, down on their knees scrubbing the floors. Curley remembered his own mother scrubbing floors on Beacon Hill and in the Back Bay, and told the cleaning women that they should be on their knees only to pray to God. He ordered long-handled mops for all the city's cleaning women, and issued an order that no scrubwoman was to get on her knees in City Hall.

It was a small, symbolic gesture, but for these women an important one. Throughout his political career, Curley fought for the interests of the city's laborers, getting them paid vacation days, shorter working hours, and other benefits. The male laborers could vote, but at the time these women could not. Pea Jacket Maguire had ignored Sarah Curley and her orphaned children after Big Michael Curley died; but James Michael Curley would be different.

Meanwhile, the great political show would go on. Curley absolutely refused to be in the same hall with his predecessor, John Fitzgerald. When Governor David Walsh, the first Irish Catholic governor of the Commonwealth, was running for re-election in 1914, Curley refused to address a rally at Tremont Temple, a popular venue for public orations of all stripes, because Fitzgerald would be in attendance. "For Governor Walsh I will go the limit, but I must draw the line at Fitzgerald-addressed rallies." If he appeared on the same platform with Fitzgerald, "I would forfeit the right to be respected." Shaking Fitzgerald's hand, Curley said, hurt his dignity.

This clash between Curley and Fitzgerald is one of the great stories in Boston's political history. Addressing the City Council in early 1915 and reviewing the record of his own administration, Curley did not mention his predecessor by name. "I would not injure my dignity by mentioning the name of the ex-mayor." What nerve! He was only ten years out of jail, which should bear at least some slight stigma. When the City Council asked to hear from the former mayor, Curley left the chamber and loudly slammed the door as Fitzgerald was being introduced.

How to account for this animosity? Curley had early on recognized that Fitzgerald was the great man in Boston politics. Curley asked a student in a Tammany Club naturalization class, "a foreigner with a name like a firecracker," about the American government.

"How are the laws of the nation made?" Curley asked.

"John F. Fitzgerald."

Curley suggested a little more reading, then asked, "How are the laws of the state made?"

"John F. Fitzgerald."

"You're consistent, anyhow. Who is president of the United States?"

"John F. Fitzgerald."

"In case there is any misunderstanding on these points," Curley told the student and the class, "I want it to be understood that John F. Fitzgerald did not discover America or drive the snakes out of Ireland."

It is claimed that Curley had driven Fitzgerald out of politics by exposing his affair with the dancer "Toodles," promising to give a series of lectures on "Great Lovers in History: From Cleopatra to Toodles." It may have been Fitzgerald's infidelity that most outraged Curley. Or it may have been Fitzgerald's failures as an administrator; though Curley had supported Fitzgerald during his first term and part of his second term, as mayor Fitzgerald was not as efficient as Curley. Or it may simply have been Curley's ambition.

"I am conducting this city on a business basis," Curley said early in his administration, "and not conducting a vaudeville show. I will leave the field clear for a vaudeville show to Mr. Fitzgerald."

Curley, master vaudevillian, denouncing Fitzgerald as a vaudevillian: this is stage entertainment at its best.

Curley was relentless in his one-upmanship. Fitzgerald was stung when Curley refused to invite him to the opening of Boston's High School of Commerce, which taught secretarial and commercial skills. Fitzgerald's response was to have himself photographed in front of the High School of Commerce, exclaiming that Curley could not prevent him from looking at the school he had built. Curley produced Board of Aldermen minutes from April 24, 1905, when Alderman Curley had first proposed building a High School of Commerce. If Fitzgerald had

July 4, 1946, Faneuil Hall: John Fitzgerald, John F. Kennedy, and Mayor Curley.
There are other photos of the three, but this is the only one in which anyone is smiling.
(Courtesy College of the Holy Cross)

anything further to say, he was, like so many others, disinclined
to continue the game of one-upmanship at which Curley
excelled.

"Honey Fitz," wrote his biographer, John Henry Cutler, about
Fitzgerald, "was a signpost who could tell you where to go, but
not always how to get there." Curley knew how to accomplish
what he was after. Curley was a great political showman, but
also a diligent and tireless administrator. Though political show-
manship overshadowed his administrative role, the day-to-day
chore of keeping the government moving was Curley's stronger
virtue. We get the idea sometimes that the campaign spectacle is
all there is to it. But the *Boston Post* in a 1934 tribute to Curley
expressed what his supporters and his foes viewed as his core
strength:

In days when city after city was defaulting its obligations, when faithful employees went without pay for months, when bare treasuries allowed of no assistance to the unfortunate, Boston stood almost alone among the large cities of the country in living up to every obligation and providing generously for all in need. No matter what the critics may say, . . . Boston kept the faith. Solvency, financial honor and consideration of those who could not help themselves went hand in hand. If this is a proud record, . . . then Mayor Curley is entitled to the tribute of a grateful people. He developed into an administrative genius. No man could possibly approach him in knowledge of the city problems. For twenty years he has been a deep and earnest student of municipal government. It is not likely we shall see a man with his vast equipment in many years to come.

The *Post* acknowledged that some saw his faults more clearly but said the faults "lie gently on him" as it bid him "not goodbye, but good luck."

Curley was, as this tribute said, an "administrative genius." In John Bantry's 1921 profile in the *Post,* the reporter pointed to the contrast between the public image of congenial and gregarious Jim Curley, and the "stern, stocky, studious looking person with the grave look of inquiry behind his heavy glasses" sitting at the desk at City Hall. Behind the desk Curley was all business, and his accomplishments demonstrate a knack for public administration. During his first three terms in City Hall, Curley built more schools than any other mayor of the city, and he abolished the "parental schools" for truant children, institutions to which habitual truants and other incorrigibles were committed. He set out to build two new branch libraries every year. He expanded Boston City Hospital and established the George Robert White Health Units throughout the city. He had sprinklers and fire alarms installed in all hospitals and hotels, and he oversaw the Fire Department's transition from horsepower to motor power. He gave all city workers a two-week paid vacation each year and established the Municipal Credit Union for city employees, who previously had had to borrow money from loan sharks to stay solvent. During the Depression years Boston, unlike other cities, paid its city workers regularly. Curley pushed successfully for a new vehicular tunnel to be built under the harbor to East Boston, and he expanded the city's transit lines, extending the East Boston tunnel to Maverick Square and the Boylston Street tunnel to Kenmore Square, and he expanded the Dorchester Rapid Transit system—three key components of the modern MBTA Blue, Green, and Red Lines. Curley shocked the Beacon Hill and Back Bay Brahmins by proposing the sale of the Public Garden, but no sale took place. He added parks in the city's densely populated neighborhoods, transforming the polluted and dangerous Old Harbor area of South Boston into Columbus Park (now Joe Moakley Park), creating fifty-six acres of new parkland. Incidentally, the baseball field in Moakley Park until recently was named for William McNary, whom Curley had beaten in 1910.

Curley also completed the Strandway, now Day Boulevard. Originally, Columbia Road and the Strandway were to have been elegant parkways continuing Frederick Law Olmsted's Emerald Necklace, a series of connected green spaces threading through the city's streets, but that project had languished since the 1890s. Curley finished the Strandway in his second term. He also built the public bathhouses at Carson Beach and at L Street, the latter now named for him. Curley promised that the L Street Bathhouse in South Boston, built at a cost of $350,000, would "provide all the advantages of a Florida trip." I heard him, at a Boston College High School dedication, call it "a finer beach than Waikiki." None of us had been to Waikiki. Who could give him an argument? Incidentally, to this day the state subsidizes the L Street Bathhouse, which nearly closed after the passage of Proposition 2½, which limits the ability of municipalities in the state to raise property taxes.

These accomplishments all required the city to spend money and hire people. Construction projects put people to work. The Parthenon in Athens is a splendid example of a W.P.A.–style project. Curley insisted that veterans be given preference for public works and city jobs. This was a good strategy. The City was

Mayor Curley lays the cornerstone of the L Street Bathhouse, now the James M. Curley Recreation Center, in South Boston, 1931. (Courtesy College of the Holy Cross)

responsible for relief payments to jobless veterans; by hiring veterans, the City saved on relief payments. Curley spent for good reason, though Republicans in state government launched a Finance Commission to keep track of the City's spending.

Curley, as both mayor and governor, persuaded public utilities to lower their rates, saving consumers a considerable amount of money. Curley mastered the kind of technical detail necessary to understand these complicated issues. As a congressman, he had listened to testimony from a lawyer and an electrical engineer representing utility companies generating hydroelectric power at Niagara Falls. The explanation of the power company's selfless work, massive investments, and puny returns dazed the other congressmen, but Curley was unimpressed. He questioned the lawyer and engineer closely about kilowatts, "just as if he knew what kilowatts were," and asked what they charged for electricity in various districts, and compared kilowatt rates for the previous ten years to show that the power companies were actually earning a 300 percent profit per year. In exasperation, the company engineer asked Curley, "Are you an electrical engineer?"

Curley was not, but as a member of Boston's Board of Aldermen he had investigated the workings of public utilities, and he had come to understand how these enterprises worked. He could put on a show in the congressional committee room (though for a hearing on public utilities it is hard to imagine much of an audience), but only because of his mastery of the utilities' technicalities.

Curley served but one term as governor, but he made the most of it. Despite the facts that the Republicans controlled the legislature and that these were tough times for the country (1935–1937), Curley persuaded banks—for the first time in twenty-five years—to reduce mortgage rates, from 6 to 5½ percent interest. This saved homeowners something like $12 million each year. He also persuaded electric companies to cut their rates, saving consumers another $2 million. Governor Curley ended the double fares that commuters from Winthrop, Chelsea, and Revere had to pay to ride the separate trolley lines into Boston; they now would pay a single fare of ten cents, rather than two ten-cent fares to transfer to the Boston line. Ten cents might not seem like a lot, but in 1935 a dime had roughly the same purchasing power as $1.50 does today—the current fare on MBTA buses.

As governor, Curley also worked to bring the New Deal's benefits to Massachusetts. Most of the New Deal programs were administered by the state—the federal government underwrote or expanded on existing programs at the state level. Something like $250 million of federal money was advanced to the state, and Curley's administration embarked on $6 million in new projects. The Civilian Conservation Corps laid out trails in the Blue Hills. There are granite curbstones all around the state, and many of these were laid during Curley's term as governor. Crews of men, who otherwise would have been jobless, were dispatched to the far corners of the Commonwealth to put in curbstones. Undoubtedly, Curley recalled that his own father had died working on a similar project.

There is a legend that Curley persuaded a bank to lend the city money by threatening to open the sewer main into the bank's vault, to dig up the street in front of the bank, or to cut off the bank's water supply. It may or may not be true. Edwin O'Connor had a more imaginative version in his novel *The Last Hurrah*. Frank Skeffington, the Curley character, suggests to a prominent banker's hapless son that he consider an appointment to be fire commissioner. Skeffington cynically tells the young man he is destined for great things and entices him to sign a letter of acceptance. Sadly concluding an interview with the banker some days later, his request for a loan rejected, Skeffington says, "By the way," and produces the son's letter of acceptance.

During the Tregor crisis in Boston, I was mustering the votes in the Senate to help Boston out, by having the state government assume a debt of $143 million the City had incurred after a lawsuit. In return, the City would give the Commonwealth two valuable properties. Mayor Kevin White again and again expressed to me his gratitude, the City's gratitude, and so on. I was "headed for something big, no question about it," he told me. I told him he was treating me the way Skeffington treated the banker's son in *The Last Hurrah*. A few days after successfully securing the city's salvation, I received a gift from Mayor White: a beautiful fire commissioner's helmet.

Curley used his persuasive power to establish health units in the city's most congested districts. Curley knew that the real estate tycoon George Robert White had the largest tax bill in Boston; he owned $5.5 million worth of property. White refused to meet with the mayor, but Curley's staff learned that the bachelor millionaire ate lunch every day, alone, at the Copley Plaza. Mayor Curley dropped in at lunch.

"I want you to give me the money to finance those health units."

"Why should I?" White asked.

"As outright philanthropy. You've got more money now than you know what to do with. You can't take it with you. Wouldn't you like to be remembered as a man who did something spectacular for the health of the people of the city? I'll chisel your name in granite all over them. I'll see to it that as long as you live, you'll never be sorry you gave me the money."

White was not persuaded, but Curley persisted, following White and explaining the dire need for health care in the city's congested slums. White showed no signs of agreeing. But when White died, he left his entire estate—$5.5 million—to the City, setting up a fund administered by the mayor, the city auditor, and the Bar Association and Chamber of Commerce presidents. Nearly every family in Boston's neighborhoods used these health units.

I remember Ed Mullin, an amputee, frequently sitting on the steps at 28 Logan Way, where I grew up. He loved the James Michael Curley of legend. No one could rival Curley. I knew this quite well by the early 1960s, when I was a state representative. I distinctly recall Ed saying, "Curley would give you anything you wanted." I thought, "Mr. Mullin, you should vote for Curley whether he is dead or alive. Go with the guy who will give you everything you ask for, though even God won't do that."

5

THE FORGOTTEN MAN

It was thought Curley had committed political suicide by endorsing Franklin Delano Roosevelt in 1932. Every other Democratic leader in the Commonwealth remained loyal to Al Smith. But Curley thought Smith had run his course in 1928 as the first Roman Catholic to be nominated for president. The nation had overwhelmingly rejected his candidacy. It would do so again.

Curley's first extended conversation with FDR came about by accident. When the Curley family returned from Italy in 1931, they happened to ride from New York to Boston on the same train as Franklin and Eleanor Roosevelt. The Roosevelts were on their way to New England to visit their sons at Groton.

Curley and Roosevelt conversed for two hours. Before the train reached Boston, Curley had decided that Franklin Roosevelt should be the Democratic nominee for president in 1932.

Ten thousand Bostonians thronged South Station when the train pulled in, coming to greet Mayor Curley and escort him with a torchlight parade to Boston Common. The crowd was gone, following Curley, before Roosevelt was wheeled through the empty station. One onlooker observed, "That's Governor Roosevelt," and an elderly woman applauded as he rose from the chair and walked—supported by an aide and a redcap—to the car. Roosevelt smiled and raised his hat to the few curious onlookers.

The next day Curley announced that Franklin Roosevelt was "the hope of the nation" and should be the next president of the

Curley was an early supporter of Franklin D. Roosevelt for president. (Courtesy Boston Public Library)

United States. Curley had made many enemies among Massachusetts Democrats. In the 1930 primary campaign Curley, then supporting John Fitzgerald, had accused one candidate, Joseph Ely, of being anti-Irish. Ely, a Yankee Protestant, responded by calling Curley a traitor to the Democratic Party and a hypocrite. "His is the desperate attempt to throw into this campaign racial prejudice to satisfy his own cruel and selfish ambition," Ely asserted. "He is a traitor to democracy, exerting all his demagogic influence to disrupt our party and further the election of his friend," the Republican governor Frank G. Allen. Ely then listed the various Democratic leaders Curley had vilified over the years: Patrick Collins; John H. Sullivan of East Boston; James Donovan ("that loved man" who Curley had said "had no visible means of support"); James A. Gallivan; John R. Murphy; General Edward A. Logan of South Boston (for whom the airport is named), "of whom Curley said he and his regiment were driven aboard the ship to across the sea at the point of a bayonet"; and finally even John Fitzgerald, whom Curley was now trying to maneuver into the governorship, "of whom he has said things to bring the blush of shame to every decent man."

Ely's charge that Curley was a hypocritical demagogue rings true. Curley responded with an attack on three of Ely's backers: disbarred Boston lawyer Dan Coakley, Larry Quigley, and Martin Lomasney. "The imposing list of so-called leaders and bosses," Curley said, "headed by such altruists as Martin M. Lomasney, Larry Quigley, and Danny Coakley, should deceive no one." Curley attacked the very idea that these bosses could deliver up the electorate. The Civil Service law had eliminated that old political order. "In the good old days, when favors were paid for political services from the federal, the state, the county, the city and town treasuries, the boss was a formidable figure. Today the picture has changed; the people can be depended upon to form their own judgment and to exercise their franchise as they believe best."

Sounding like a Good Government reformer, Curley said that the "bosses today are only bogeymen; they are in no sense to be feared." Curley thought the bosses' support would work against Ely, whereas a true "spirit of gratitude" would inspire the many "beneficiaries of that kindly, generous, cheerful character who has graced the arena of Democratic politics in Massachusetts for more than four decades" to support John Fitzgerald.

This is truly vintage Curley—attacking the ward bosses while pushing to have one of the biggest of them—John Fitzgerald—elected governor.

On the night before the primary in 1930, Curley and State Party Chairman Frank J. "Daisy" Donahue were both scheduled to appear on the same radio station. Curley listened in the station's waiting room as Donahue charged that Curley had really not done all he could in 1928 to elect Al Smith (who was campaigning for Ely in Massachusetts). In the campaign's final weeks Curley had barely campaigned at all, and he had refused to speak at nighttime rallies.

Curley was enraged. He had indeed curtailed his campaign activities in 1928. His wife Mary was slowly dying of cancer. He was at her side throughout her ordeal.

Curley waited for Donahue to come out of the studio. Details vary on what Curley said, but as he rushed at the diminutive party chairman, the gist of his remarks was, "I'll get you, you son of a bitch, if it's the last thing I ever do." Dan Coakley's son stepped between Donahue and Curley, taking hits in the knee and groin as Donahue fled the room.

Curley composed himself as he walked into the studio.

"Mr. Donahue knows why I did not leave my home at night during that campaign," Curley began. He explained to the radio audience that he been on "a more important though sadder mission" than electioneering. He did not mention his wife's struggle with cancer, or her death. He said he was shocked that anyone would bring such a sacred matter into a political campaign.

Here we have within the space of a few minutes the many sides of Curley: the man whose most personal and sacred duty is to his wife; the street fighter who will punch out an opponent; and the campaigner who can make poetry out of a political address as well as push demagoguery to new depths. How is he to be defined?

Ely won the nomination. All expected fireworks when Curley strode into the state convention. But a gracious Curley beamed to all as he mounted the rostrum to offer Ely his congratulations. For his part, Ely jokingly referred to himself as a "hick from the sticks," one of the kinder things Curley had called him. To show there were no hard feelings, Curley presented Ely with a campaign contribution in the form of a check for one thousand dollars. Ely's smile disappeared when he looked at the check. Curley had made it out not to Ely or the state Democratic Party, but to Boston's Democratic City Committee.

It is small wonder that Massachusetts Democrats hoped to bury Curley in 1932. Governor Ely became Al Smith's most fervent supporter. Curley and Jimmy Roosevelt, Roosevelt's son living in Cambridge, campaigned throughout the state, but they came up empty. No one would rent Curley a hall for a rally; he found no crowds to address. Even the Ancient Order of Hibernians dropped him as a member. His apostasy from Al Smith seemed to be suicidal.

Ely and the Smith forces controlled the Massachusetts delegation to the Democratic National Convention, and they even denied Curley a place on it. Curley certainly did not count himself out. At the end of the primary campaign, Roosevelt had 660 delegates, which was a majority, but a nominee needed two-thirds, or 770 votes, to win. Roosevelt's opponents—Al Smith with 150 delegates, John Nance Garner, controlling Texas and California, and a variety of "favorite son" candidates—hoped to block Roosevelt on the first ballot and nominate someone else.

Ely himself placed Smith's name in nomination, a chore Roosevelt had performed in 1920, 1924, and 1928. Ely delivered what one observer called the best convention speech in half a century (most convention speeches are, well, conventional). Not only was it a brilliant speech, but Ely delivered it with such passion that he instantly became a national figure and a rumored candidate for higher office.

Ely's speech, though, was greatly overshadowed by the appearance of one of Puerto Rico's delegates, seated, by chance, directly behind the all-Smith Massachusetts delegation. "Alcalde Jaime Miguel Curleo" sat smiling, and when Puerto Rico was called, that familiar voice delivered the island's vote to Franklin Roosevelt. Curley had arrived in Chicago without even a visitor's pass to the convention, but he learned that a vacancy had—or might—arise in the Puerto Rico delegation. He gallantly offered to fill it. His Massachusetts rivals had written Curley out of the story, but he returned.

Curley circulated through the convention hall—"I am really surprised to find so many people here whom I know and with whom I can talk on behalf of the Roosevelt cause," he said. He had a knack for finding familiar faces, and also for finding microphones and reporters.

After the nominating speeches, the delegates began voting—and for twelve hours they continued. After three ballots, and a full night of voting, Roosevelt was still eighty-six votes short. What would happen next? The convention was adjourned, Roosevelt's supporters fearing the worst.

Curley's dramatic appearance as a delegate from Puerto Rico. (Courtesy Boston Public Library)

For Roosevelt, the key to the problem was William Randolph Hearst, who was at home in California running his media empire. Hearst, a native New Yorker, backed Garner, probably remembering that Smith had snubbed him when Hearst sought a Senate seat from New York. Another Smith adversary, William Gibbs McAdoo, chaired the California delegation. McAdoo and Smith had fought one another for the Democratic nomination in 1924, and they deadlocked the convention for 128 ballots before the weary party nominated a Wall Street lawyer named John W. Davis, who was unceremoniously drubbed in November by Calvin Coolidge. McAdoo and Hearst would not tolerate Smith, but they had no real affection for Franklin Roosevelt, either, and Roosevelt's people were reluctant to call Hearst on their candidate's behalf.

There are several conflicting stories about what happened. According to James Michael Curley, who did get along with Hearst, it was Curley who personally called Hearst, persuading the publisher to sway California to Roosevelt; in turn, Curley persuaded Roosevelt to name Garner as his running mate.

But Curley was not the only Roosevelt backer with a line to Hearst. Joseph P. Kennedy, at the time a New York financier with significant interests in the movie industry, was one of Roosevelt's chief financial backers. Kennedy knew Hearst, and he reportedly called Hearst on Roosevelt's behalf. Kennedy, son of an East Boston ward boss and son-in-law of Curley's longtime rival John Fitzgerald, apparently despised Curley.

Which is the true story? Curley was fond of exaggerating his own role in events, though his story is plausible. We do know that after the election Roosevelt rewarded Curley with precisely nothing, whereas Joe Kennedy became chair of the Securities and Exchange Commission and ambassador to England.

At any rate, on the convention's second night, the California delegation's chair, William Gibbs McAdoo, went to the podium to announce that "California came here tonight to nominate a president of the United States. She did not come here to deadlock this convention or engage in another devastating contest like that of 1924." He glanced down at Al Smith, a reminder that eight years earlier McAdoo and Smith had deadlocked at the convention, hopelessly splitting the party and losing the election to the Republican incumbent. "When a man comes into a convention with almost seven hundred votes . . ."

This provoked a demonstration—Roosevelt's supporters rose and roared and marched through the aisles for half an hour cheering, and our hero Jaime Miguel Curleo carried Puerto Rico's banner triumphantly through the hall—before it quieted enough for McAdoo to declare, "California—forty-four votes for Roosevelt!" which was followed by another half hour of pandemonium.

Roosevelt won the nomination. The next night, after an Alabama congressman put Garner's name in nomination for the vice presidency, Curleo rose to give a seconding speech.

"In conformity with an old Spanish custom," he began, "as one of the 'forgotten men' I was admitted as a delegate from the beautiful island of Puerto Rico." He said he had the honor as a member of Congress to serve four years on the Foreign Relations Committee with the "distinguished, brilliant, and able son of Texas, John N. Garner."

Turning then to the main theme of the campaign, the "forgotten man," Curley went on.

> *Much has been said of the "forgotten man." Naturally, I have been a bit interested in him myself. Some have asked who is he and where is he, and I have made it my business to make inquiry. To those who are unfamiliar with his existence, I want to say that within the last thirty days he could be found within the shadow of the national Capitol at Washington to the number of 15,000 sleeping in the open. To those who might visit the greatest industrial city in the whole world, the city of Detroit, he might be found with his dependents to the number of 600,000, out of a population of 2,000,000, or almost one in every three of the men, women, and children in the city of Detroit. To those who might journey to the richest city in the entire world, the city of New York, he would find the "forgotten man" and his dependents to the number of 1,300,000 subsisting on public charity, victims in the richest land of the whole world of Hooverism.*

Garner's nomination was an anticlimax to the drama of Roosevelt's, but both were overshadowed by the real drama of Roosevelt's appearance at the convention—the first candidate to accept the nomination in person at the nominating convention.

There were no public opinion polls in 1932, and though now we see Roosevelt's election as a certainty, some thought he would not win in November. The journalist H. L. Mencken thought the Democrats had actually nominated their weakest candidate, and Mencken was not alone in thinking Roosevelt a lightweight.

Curley returns triumphantly from the Chicago convention, 1932. (Courtesy Boston Public Library)

Curley and the Massachusetts delegates went home—on separate trains—to begin the campaign. Curley had left Boston a "forgotten man," written off as politically dead by the rest of the Massachusetts party. But he returned to Boston on July 4 to a hero's welcome—banners welcoming "the delegate from Puerto Rico" hung from the streets between North Station and Boston Common, and crowds lining the streets shouted, "Hurrah for Puerto Rico!" At the Parkman Bandstand, Jimmy Roosevelt joined Curley, who began his speech, "Señors and Señoritas," and predicted that Roosevelt would win, saying,

> *[Roosevelt] is the only hope of the "forgotten man," and the "forgotten men" by the millions will rise throughout the nation to win work and wages through the victory of Franklin D. Roosevelt.*

The faith of the fathers lost during the past four years gives promise of being revived through real leadership in the person of Franklin D. Roosevelt. To him those Americans who have wandered helplessly in the shadow of adversity in the past four years, and to him every thoughtful citizen regardless of party affiliation who has viewed the growing murmurs of discontent with downright fear, looks for deliverance.

The election of Franklin D. Roosevelt will mark a new day in the life of America. To him we look for the adoption of an economic program that will restore both faith and opportunity to the American people. Under his leadership we look forward with confidence, born of a knowledge of his past work, for a brighter, a more happy, and a more prosperous day in the life of America when the scriptural admonition, "I am my brother's keeper," will become a reality rather than, as in the present day, a mockery.

Back at his City Hall office, Curley placed Puerto Rico's flag between the flags of Boston and Massachusetts.

Curley's power as an orator had impressed the movie mogul Jack Warner, who invited the mayor to New York to film his "Forgotten Man" speech. Curley arrived without the text of his speech, and the director shook his head at the prospect of filming an actor with no script. But Curley, after more than three decades of speaking in public, hardly needed a script, and in one take he spoke for eleven minutes on his search for "the forgotten man."

I have made it my business to ascertain if such an individual really existed in America, and have endeavored to ascertain the underlying causes for his presence in our midst, and I found upon investigation that he was one of the products of the industrial depression with which America has been visited during the now nearly four years that have passed.

I learned that in 1930 he could be found in America to number of three and one half millions; in 1931 his number had grown to seven and one half millions, and in this year of grace, 1932, he numbered in excess of ten millions of men in America; men without employment; men without prospect of employment, yet—strange to behold—patient and still patriotic.

Curley set out to find the forgotten man's daily habits, and in "Times Square, New York, the richest city in the whole world," he found "every evening at 12 o'clock, winter and summer," the forgotten man and two thousand others gathered for an opportunity "to secure just a little sustenance to keep body and soul together until he attended once more the breadline on the following night." In Chicago Curley "discovered him in the vacant lots to the number of 1,200, sleeping in packing cases and in the morning crawling forth like an animal." In Washington, D.C., he found the "ranks swollen with recruits from every section of America," as the "Bonus Marchers," jobless and homeless veterans of the World War who wanted their promised bonuses in 1932, rather than 1942, as had been promised in 1918. Curley saw the Bonus Marchers gather on the steps of the Capitol "on the very day that Congress rejected the proposal which he sought—the payment of the bonus." He noted that the marchers, instead of condemning public officials for denying them their due, "joined together and sang, 'My Country 'tis of thee; sweet land of liberty,' exhibiting a sublime patriotism under most trying circumstances unexcelled in the history of our country."

Curley called for a National Industrial Planning Commission to study the causes of the Depression and to plan for a solution, not only to end the Depression but to prevent future ones. He also called for shortening the workweek to five days (rather than the typical six of the time) because the American worker had become more productive, able to produce in seven months the goods that previously had taken twelve to produce.

"I believe we are all of one mind that the machine, which we hoped would be the servant of man in America, has become the master, and the workingman the slave of the machine." Industrialization and automation had made American factories more productive, but at the cost of eliminating the need for American labor and making the American workingman the "forgotten man" in the shadows of prosperity. Franklin D. Roosevelt had the vision to see these fundamental problems in the American economy; he was the "one hope for the disappearance from the life of

America of the 'forgotten man' and the return once more of equality of opportunity for all men living under the stars and stripes of our country."

The director was astonished that Curley could so effortlessly fill eleven minutes of film. "Eleven minutes!" Curley exclaimed; "I could have gone on for eleven days." That fall Curley's "Forgotten Man" speech played in thousands of theaters throughout the nation. Curley himself in September embarked on a nationwide speaking tour: ten thousand miles through twenty-three states, making over a hundred speeches—in public halls and on the radio—in thirty days. After a send-off from Boston on September 1, Curley spoke to 5,000 who paid admission to hear him in South Bend, Indiana, where he was also a guest at a dinner at Notre Dame; then in Milwaukee 7,500 people paid to hear him speak. After that speech a delegation of several hundred socialists announced their support for Roosevelt. Curley delivered a Labor Day address to 7,500 people at Chicago's Soldier's Field, carried throughout the land by radio. In Portland, Oregon, Curley spoke to another 7,500 at the American Legion Convention.

"Mayor Curley is the phenomenon of American political life," one reporter wrote. "Though his formal education extended only as far as the sixth [sic] grade, he uses faultless grammar and diction, spiced with an authentic Back Bay accent. There are classical and historical allusions through his speeches."

How authentic the "Back Bay accent" was is debatable; what is not is that Curley was a most effective campaigner. Had he been only a demagogue, as his opponents claimed, or the rascal king, as others dubbed him, it is doubtful the Roosevelt campaign would have sent him on this national odyssey. Ten thousand Bostonians gathered to greet Curley when he returned home in October—six months after he was snubbed, shunned, and written off as politically dead. Now he was a national figure, and he was on hand at the end of October to greet Roosevelt during the nominee's triumphant tour of New England.

At the end, Roosevelt carried forty-two of the forty-eight states in the nation, sweeping Hoover and the Republicans out of office.

The campaign seemed to augur great things for Curley in a Roosevelt administration. But it turned out that the campaign itself—Curley's first national tour—would be the high point of his career; he never went much further after this, the possible reasons for which I will get to shortly. Curley expected a Cabinet post—in fact, he hoped to replace another Massachusetts man, Charles Francis Adams, as secretary of the navy. Curley had long been an advocate of naval spending, having supported expansion of the Charlestown Navy Yard and the Port of Boston.

He and his daughter Mary traveled to Warm Springs, Georgia, to meet with the president-elect. Mary admonished her father not to get his hopes up when she saw him doodling, drawing an admiral's hat on a magazine he was reading. Roosevelt seemed to promise the navy, but would have to clear it with others first. The Curleys went home.

6

THE LAST HURRAH

By 1932 the tide in Curley's eventful life had reached its flood, and it now would begin to ebb. He was fifty-eight years old; his wife, Mary, had died; Standish Wilcox had died suddenly on January 2, 1933. Curley lost his closest friends, and the only ones who could restrain his penchant for mischief.

The afternoon of Wilcox's funeral, former president Calvin Coolidge died at his home in Northampton, his last words being "I no longer fit in with these times." At Coolidge's funeral Curley ran into Jimmy Roosevelt, who told him that the navy post was out; but he mentioned the possibility of an ambassadorship.

Weeks passed, and there was no word from Washington. Certainly, the incoming administration had more pressing concerns than what position to give Mayor Curley, the national economy being in full collapse. But it also became clear that Curley would not be acceptable to other Massachusetts Democrats, such as Senator Walsh, who was becoming a key Roosevelt ally in Congress. Curley traveled to Washington for the inauguration, and President Roosevelt mentioned France, but Curley demurred, having heard from a previous ambassador of the expenses of living in Paris. What about Rome?

Curley had prepared in advance. On his 1931 trip to Rome, he had negotiated a truce among King Victor Emmanuel III, Premier Benito Mussolini, and Pope Pius XI—over Mussolini's attempt to disband the Catholic Boy Scouts and force all young Italian men into his own fascist youth organization. Expecting difficulties, and sensing that Roosevelt preferred duplicity to disappointment (Roosevelt was perhaps the greatest politician of them all), Curley had wired the king, the premier, and the pope to see if any of them objected to his appointment. All wired back that Curley would be acceptable.

Curley had the cables in his pocket when he went to the State Department. He was told that the president was very disappointed that objections in Italy prevented Curley's being sent to Rome.

Who objected? Curley wanted to know. Was it the premier?

Yes, it may have been Mussolini.

Curley produced his cable from the premier's office saying Curley would be acceptable.

Then it must have been the king.

Curley produced his cable from the palace.

Then perhaps it was the pope, after all.

Curley lay his cable from the Vatican on the table.

No more needed to be said. Curley knew he would not be going to Rome.

After he returned to Boston, the administration publicly announced that Curley would be appointed American ambassador to Poland. Warsaw was not Rome. Though the administration indicated Poland's importance, and one Boston editorial writer expected that Curley would pave the Polish corridor, he declined the appointment.

At least one newspaper praised Curley for choosing to stay in Boston, addressing the difficult task of governing the city in the midst of a major depression, over the more glamorous role of an ambassador. Back in Boston, Curley was determined to put the forgotten man back to work, which he did through public works projects, such as putting the trolley lines underneath Kenmore Square, rather than have the Commonwealth Avenue tunnel open into the square itself; and building a new tunnel under the harbor.

In digging the new subway tunnel, the contractors shattered a water pipe near the General Equipment Corporation, flooding

Curley came to feel betrayed by Roosevelt. (Courtesy Boston Public Library)

the basement. The insurance company paid off General Equipment, but it then sued the city for $70,000 in damages. The jurors awarded the company $129,000, which the judge set aside. The insurer now was willing to settle for $20,000, but for reasons unexplained, the city paid $85,000. The Finance Commission, always on the watch for Curley's malfeasance, discovered that though the city had indeed allocated $85,000 in this case, the insurance company received only $20,000. Where was the rest?

It also appeared that the city treasurer, Edmund Dolan, was operating the Legal Securities Company, a stock-and-bond outfit, on the side. The Finance Commission, which Curley called Peeping Toms, was investigating Dolan.

Curley announced he would run for governor. Joseph Ely was retiring; the Republican candidate would be Gaspar Griswold Bacon. Bacon had been president of the State Senate; he had been elected lieutenant governor in 1930, receiving more votes statewide than any other Republican candidate had up to that time.

Bacon wanted to meet Curley face-to-face and defeat him. But 1934 would be a Democratic year (it was one of the few times the party that held the White House actually picked up seats in Congress); and Curley painted the mildly progressive and competent Bacon as an elitist Republican. Saying his name, Gaspar—Griswold—Bacon, emphasizing each of the three last names his opponent bore, Curley reminded his listeners that Bacon's father, who had briefly been Theodore Roosevelt's secretary of state, had also been part of J. P. Morgan's investment firm. "While many of the citizens of Massachusetts were on welfare lists, Gaspar Griswold Bacon was on J. P. Morgan's preferred list." The facts that it was Bacon's father who had been on Morgan's preferred list back in 1894, and that Gaspar Griswold Bacon himself had never worked for Morgan, were irrelevant.

A Gaspar Griswold Bacon look-alike would cruise through the streets in a limousine, admonishing state work crews to "stop leaning on their shovels." But it was not all vaudeville. Curley had a record of delivering, and he promised to continue as governor. He would establish a state planning board, build roads and bridges, put people to work; but he would also take care of the people in the shadows. He pledged better treatment for the mentally ill, who in some cases were "treated worse than wild beasts. Even animals in our forest preserves are protected against fire. I want proper segregation for the hopeless and enlightened treatment for the curables. That's one reform that I am certain is coming. Even the most stilted and pompous spokesman of the old regime will not dare to obstruct it, and I want to make sure that no one in the state starves."

Curley swept into office. He would serve one two-year term as governor, but he would not win another election until 1942.

Curley was sixty when he was elected governor, though he had the same frenetic energy he'd had at thirty: working sixteen, eighteen hours a day, meeting with the hundreds who streamed into the governor's office, putting people to work—he found jobs for sixty thousand people on public works projects—building roads, tunnels, bridges, hospitals, and having teams of men laying curbstones throughout the state.

Spring floods in 1936 restored Curley's waning popularity. He oversaw relief efforts, reconstruction of washed-out bridges, rebuilding of roads. Had he sought reelection, he would have won in a walk. It was a Democratic year—Roosevelt would carry every state but Maine and Vermont—but Curley had set his sights on the U.S. Senate. The Republicans were running Henry Cabot Lodge Jr., grandson of the great Senator Lodge who had blocked the League of Nations. Curley now was sixty-two, and Lodge was only thirty-four. Curley mocked Lodge as "Little Boy Blue," a political neophyte, and without much of a record. Lodge had been Washington correspondent for the *Boston Transcript* in 1923, then wrote for the *New York Herald Tribune* before returning to the Brahmin enclave of Nahant, which sent him to the state legislature for two terms in the early 1930s. With not much to say against Henry Cabot Lodge other than that he was young, Curley ran against his grandfather. "The only problem with Henry Cabot," Curley would say, "is that he thinks there are only two people in the world, both named Henry Cabot." At rally after rally Curley reminded his audience that in 1915 the senior Lodge had tried to block Louis D. Brandeis's confirmation to the Supreme Court. The obvious implication was that Lodge was anti-Semitic, as well as an opponent of one of the country's leading liberals. Curley ignored the fact that in 1913 Congressman Curley had tried to prevent President Wilson from naming Brandeis to his Cabinet.

John Hynes, a loyal member of Curley's team, later to be city clerk and later still to beat Curley, wrote a little pamphlet, *This Man Curley,* as a campaign piece. Hynes listed in detail all Curley's significant accomplishments as governor of the Commonwealth—and it was an impressive record.

Curley was confident in 1936. Too confident. Though Democrats swept every statewide office in Massachusetts—Treasurer Charles Hurley was elected governor—Lodge beat Curley by

Jimmy Roosevelt and Curley march to the 1936 Democratic Convention. Hoping for election to the Senate, Curley also anticipated running for president in 1940. (Courtesy College of the Holy Cross)

136,000 votes and began a long and distinguished career on the national stage.

This was a low point for Curley, but he was ever optimistic. As he prepared to leave the State House for an uncertain future, Curley secured a degree of personal happiness by marrying Gertrude Dennis, a widow with two grown sons. Curley and Gertrude Dennis actually married on the morning he left office. Bishop Francis Spellman—later a cardinal and archbishop of New York—celebrated their wedding at Boston College's St. Mary's Chapel at ten in the morning; the governor returned to the State House, where he prepared for his ceremonial exit. By tradition going back to 1883, the retiring governor departs alone through the State House's front doors and down the steps, returning to the role of private citizen as he blends into the crowds on the Common. But at the bottom of the steps the new Mrs. Curley met the retiring governor. His marriage and dramatic exit from office assured a front-page story in the next day's papers.

Curley decided in 1937 to run again for mayor of Boston. This time his opponent was a young and talented member of his own loose machine, Maurice Tobin. Tobin was thirty-six (nearly thirty years younger than Curley) and handsome; Curley said afterward it was not an election but a beauty contest. Tobin was popular with many people from Curley's organization, but more important, he had the support of a lot of people who hated Curley. The publisher of the *Boston Post,* Clifton Carberry, plugged away for Tobin as the exemplar of a youthful new generation. Carberry really poured it on in the *Post,* making Tobin, and his attractive young family, the center of attention. Pictures of Tobin's daughter and his aged mother, who was about Curley's age, filled the paper.

This election gave Edwin O'Connor the idea for his novel *The Last Hurrah,* as Tobin supposedly represented something new in politics, against the old style that Curley stood for. O'Connor tells the story of the election through the eyes of Frank Skeffington's (Curley's) nephew Adam Caulfield, a representative of the rising assimilated generation. Adam's wife is apolitical; her father has always despised Skeffington. Adam himself is skeptical, but the old buccaneer encourages him to come and observe the campaign. Adam finds himself drawn into the spectacle, and into the personality of Skeffington. He also finds that those who know Skeffington best, those who respect him the most, are not his hangers-on and dependents, but his lifelong opponents. The business leaders hate him for his shrewdness, his ability to see through their self-serving ploys, and his unyielding commitment to the city. The cardinal in the book, modeled of course on William Cardinal O'Connell, for years has been embarrassed by Skeffington; now he conspires with the others to rid the city of him, but he quietly rues the undeniable truth that the reform candidate, his candidate to oust Skeffington, is a soulless empty suit.

Tobin and later John Hynes were accepted in places where Curley never could be. The business community embraced them, the press embraced them. Anything would be better than Curley. After all, when Curley was mayor, friend and foe had to concede that it was in fact Curley who was mayor. He thought his own thoughts and came to his own conclusions. His successors were loved by the local press. They shared their power with those to whom they were beholden. They were good politicians, successful politicians who unashamedly curried the favor of the business known as the press. They would be less battered and less controversial than Curley, whose independence of spirit was viewed as an attitude of defiance. No hint of defiance would be discerned in the new, approved variety of politician. The press saw itself as the vox populi. Curley understood himself, however, to be the bona fide vox populi by virtue of his having been elected to his post by the people. If the press would rule, then let it stand for election, rather than rule through intimidation of those who are in fact chosen by the electorate.

If the press's animosity was a response to some negative aspect of Curley's character, that would be one thing. I think it had more to do with something about Curley himself—whether you liked or disliked him, he was running his own ship. He was not micromanaging every little detail, but he did indeed represent the interests of the larger community. If the interests of the larger community came into conflict with the shakers and the movers, then Curley would not be budged.

You can see how the campaign was going by looking at the *Post* on the day before the election. There on page 10 is a Tobin ad: "The Dawn of a New Era for Boston," with the handsome face of Maurice Tobin rising in the sun over the city skyline. "Youth sweeps on to Victory in Boston's greatest triumph for clean, honest government," the ad says. "Boston looks to the New Generation which will again put our city in the foreground." Then a real clincher for the candidate: "In every great intellectual and political movement youth has played an important part." There is a pattern here—youth is important. This is not the first, or the last, time we have heard about a "New Boston," though we have yet to hear about the specific role Maurice Tobin has played in any of the great intellectual or political movements of the day. The final line—"Youth marches on!"—I suppose is always true. Youth not only marches on, but eventually ages and dies.

In addition to these stirring platitudes, the ad offered the substance of the "New Era for Boston" program, all sufficiently vague. Tobin favored lower taxes and clean and honest government. Who does not? He favored a "scientific study" of the relief problem, "with possibility of obtaining direct aid from national government to care for abnormal relief load now carried by city, but city to retain control over expenditures." Study the problem; find some way to get the national government to send the money, but the city will decide how to spend it. It could happen.

The candidate really goes out on a limb on the City Hospital issue. "I favor study of hospital needs of city." How cautious can a man be? He will study the issue. Perhaps a blue-ribbon commission will be appointed?

The pièce de résistance came on election morning, November 2. The front page carried a cartoon of a young man and woman, "The Boston Younger Voter," casting their ballots for Maurice Tobin, "For a New Deal," while above the masthead ran a bulletin:

> *VOTERS OF BOSTON: Cardinal O'Connell, in speaking to the Catholic Alumni Association, said, "The walls are raised against honest men in civic life." You can break down those walls by voting for an honest, clean, competent young man, MAURICE TOBIN, today. He will redeem the city and take it out of the hands of those who have been responsible for graft and corruption. MAURICE TOBIN can win with the help of those who have had enough of these selfish oldtimers. Too long they have been supported by the tax payers. They have had more than enough.*

Here is the measure of the *Post*'s honesty. The cardinal had uttered the ten quoted words some six years before, in a totally different context. But it appears to be an urgent endorsement. The newspaper was given away free of charge to tens of thousands of churchgoers as they emerged from Mass on that All Soul's Day morning.

The *Post* carried the day. Tobin received 102,276 votes to Curley's 80,026. Curley's strength was sapped by the presence on the ballot of District Attorney William Foley, who received 28,773 votes. The incumbent, Malcolm Nichols, garnered 55,137 votes.

Maurice Tobin and the powerful *Post* were now the mayor. And this shameful act of deceit would slip into the political lore of Boston. The message was clear. Make your peace with the press or risk such savagery. Think of the words of Edmund Burke: "Your representative owes you not his industry only but his judgment, and he betrays instead of serving you if he sacrifices it to your opinion." It is a political virtue, honest judgment. It must be accompanied by the virtue of courage. For many Bostonians, Curley with his imperfections was to be preferred over those who had mortgaged themselves to the unscrupulous media business. But the press ultimately will prevail, because it has more power and will stoop lower.

The *Post* continued to pour it on for Tobin, referring to him on the day after the election as being "in the Horatio Alger Tradition" and emphasizing Tobin's humble roots, hard work, diligent effort. These attributes, of course, are readily recognized as common to most of the men and women of that time, and any time, as well as to Curley himself.

Curley ran for governor again the next year. He faced the Republican Leverett Saltonstall, an upstanding fellow—a raw-boned and upright Yankee who had few enemies. Curley made a fateful attempt at humor in this gubernatorial campaign. Saltonstall—one of his ancestors had come on the *Arbella* with other members of the Massachusetts Bay Company in 1630—was not a handsome man. Some said he looked like an Indian named Horseface. The *Boston Transcript* said that he had a "Back Bay name and a South Boston face." Curley could not resist a crack. "He may have a South Boston face, but he doesn't dare show it in South Boston." Saltonstall took the challenge—the next morning he strolled up Broadway in South Boston, chatting with people on the street, visiting the taverns and coffeehouses, socializing at playgrounds. Now someone said he "talked like Back Bay, but sounded like South Boston." "I may have a South Boston face, but I am not two-faced," he said, and thereafter instead of being called "Lev," he was "Salty," and he was elected a member of the Charitable Irish. I don't think he ever missed a St. Patrick's Day Parade or Breakfast, and he handed Curley his third straight defeat.

Saltonstall's son and I served together in the State Senate, and whenever we would be speaking of some historical matter, Bill Saltonstall would say, "Be sure to remember my father." He may have felt his father was not appreciated, a common sentiment among families of political figures.

I did once help Bill Saltonstall get reelected. I went to his district, in Manchester-by-the-Sea, to speak about a bill I had filed to open beaches to the public. I told the audience that because of Bill Saltonstall's skill as a parliamentarian, my proposal, which Bill's constituents opposed, was stalled in the senate. I think that I touched a sensitive chord when I pointed out that the people of Manchester-by-the-Sea were welcome to use Boston Common any day of the week, and that the people of Boston should be able to use Singing Beach in Manchester. I could see the audience stiffen. But again I reminded them of Bill Saltonstall's legislative tenacity. They cheered him lustily as I stood there. As Curley had helped elect Leverett Saltonstall, I more deliberately provided help to his son, a splendid public servant.

7

I'D DO IT AGAIN

Curley had now entered the time Samuel Johnson wrote of in "The Vanity of Human Wishes," "Love ends with Hope, the sinking Statesman's Door/Pours in the Morning Worshiper no more," when the portraits are taken down and the good works forgotten. O'Connor in *The Last Hurrah* had known that the 1937 race would make a fitting end—he has Skeffington die shortly afterward.

But Curley survived, though with serious financial problems. He was now approaching seventy, and his role in the General Equipment Company insurance settlement was coming back to haunt him. He was judged to have improperly received part of the payment and to owe the city close to $43,000; he had to pay $500 a week for eighty-six weeks or go to jail.

Legend has it that one morning soon after the judgment, a line formed outside Curley's Jamaicaway home, and from across the city came anonymous friends with small gifts of money. These were the people whom Curley had helped in his long career—with a job, a bag of groceries, or maybe just a kind word—and now they came to do what they could in turn. All day they came, and the next, and the next. Over the next month fifteen thousand people came to his door, and many more sent donations through the mail. This helped to keep Curley afloat. It is hard to imagine a similar turnout for any public official today.

In 1941 Curley ran again for mayor. Tobin had cut city spending, eliminating the health units in East Boston and Charlestown, and though an early poll by the *Post* gave Tobin a lead of 57,000 votes, in the end the totals were 125,786 for Tobin, 116,430 for Curley. Curley was still a formidable force. In 1942 he saw an opportunity to run for Congress—not from his old seat, but from the Charlestown/East Boston/Cambridge district. East Boston and Charlestown had long been his two best wards—he had carried both in 1937. The incumbent was a one-term Democrat, Thomas Hopkinson Eliot. Eliot's grandfather had been president of Harvard, but he was more than just another Brahmin. He was probably a better candidate than our hero. As a young lawyer in the Department of Labor, Eliot had been the principal author of the Social Security Act of 1935, and he had been the first counsel to the newly created Social Security Board. Eliot had done a remarkable job working with Congress to get the Social Security Act passed, and then to make sure that Social Security would be a viable program. He was a very good lawyer and a capable public servant. It is men like Eliot, men of dedication and talent, who do in fact sacrifice by devoting themselves to public service. The survival of our democracy depends on such people.

There was some irony in this campaign. In *The Last Hurrah* a critical observer explains why Skeffington lost in 1937: "All you have to remember is one name: Roosevelt." Roosevelt "put the skids" to Curley, and "destroyed the old-time boss" by "taking away the source of power." Roosevelt took the "handouts out of the local hands. A few little things like Social Security, Unemployment Insurance, and the like." Not only had Eliot drafted the Social Security Act, he had also drafted the federal program that pushed states to adopt unemployment insurance. So in 1942, there were two different visions of the future, represented by Eliot and Curley. Curley charged Eliot with being too far to the left: "Curley or Communism" was one slogan, and Curley was elected. Even before the votes were counted, Curley was in Washington conferring with John McCormack, the longtime representative from Massachusetts who was then House Majority Leader.

Eliot continued to serve the public; he ran again in 1944 (unsuccessfully), served on a number of wartime boards, then practiced law in Boston before moving to Missouri to teach at Washington University, which he eventually served as dean and chancellor. He also was president of the Salzburg Seminar in American Studies, and after his retirement he returned to Cambridge to teach at Buckingham, Browne, and Nichols School. Eliot is a man worthy of emulation.

Curley's two terms in Congress kept him out of danger of arrest for failing to make his $500 weekly payment, but they also took him out of the public eye back home. By December 1944 he was able, with the help of his constituents, to pay off the sum he owed the city; but then the problem with the Engineers Group surfaced again.

At this same time Curley planned another run for mayor of Boston. Tobin had been elected governor; John Kerrigan, the president of the City Council, was acting as mayor and was a candidate for the office. I knew Kerrigan well; I was impressed that he would never spend a quarter on his reelection. He would go out and talk to people, starting off from his home on East 8th Street, walking up Dorchester Street in the morning. Because he would recognize old friends sitting in the taverns on Dorchester Street, he would stop to say hello. But he broke that habit when he heard that people going by on the bus would see him emerging from a tavern and say, "Boy, Kerrigan is getting an early start." Curley trounced Kerrigan in the 1945 mayor's race by a two-to-one margin.

So in January 1946 Curley prepared to become mayor for the fourth time, and he also prepared for his trial in Washington, D.C. It would result in Curley's spending five months in the federal penitentiary at Danbury, Connecticut. He came back to Boston the day before Thanksgiving to a tumultuous welcome at South Station. During his absence the city had been capably administered by the city clerk, John Hynes, loyal to Curley and loyal to the city. Hynes, in fact, had been made the permanent city clerk—he had life tenure in the office provided he never ran for mayor.

Curley with Gertrude Dennis Curley, whom he married on his last day as governor, as he is inaugurated for his fourth mayoral term. (Courtesy Boston Public Library)

Curley returned to City Hall on the morning after Thanksgiving, and as he left for lunch he could not resist another one-liner. "I have accomplished more in one morning than the clerk has done in five months."

Hynes was a mild-mannered man; this was one of the few times his family saw him angry. That night he resolved he would run for mayor, and in 1949 he did. He beat Curley in an upset. Changes in the city charter meant another mayor's race in 1951; again Curley ran, and again Hynes beat him.

I was working as a bartender at Boston College when it sponsored the Citizens Seminars in the early 1950s. Their purpose was to get together the smart people, the doctors, bankers, lawyers, many of whom had left the city for the suburbs. Now they formed the New Boston Committee to plan ways to improve the city they had left. Though some of the changes may have been salutary, and there is nothing wrong with public-spirited citizens offering their opinions, we should look to the results of these seminars—the demolition of the West End, the building of the Central Artery, the elimination of Scollay Square—and judge the results. No one likes the new City Hall or City Hall Plaza, and no one dislikes the old City Hall on School Street.

Curley was always distrustful of the New Boston Committee. To him, they were just another bunch of Goo-Goos. He did battle with Jerome Rappaport, Hynes's assistant and one of the creators of the New Boston Committee, and those who were eager to transform the city. Soon a government of elected officials was replaced by a government of experts. To whom does one appeal in the face of a bureaucracy's decision to raze an entire neighborhood?

Such government action, clearly unjust, counterproductive, unnecessary, would be imposed on the Boston citizenry to the loud applause of the unaffected proponents, who were smugly well intentioned for the most part. The strong political leadership of the past was no longer in view.

I remember tending bar at the B.C. Club, seeing the various parties to the New Boston coming to present their plans for a new city. They seemed—the lawyers, the social planners, the professors—an enterprising and ambitious bunch, and it struck me how they all were jockeying for position, preening to present themselves as the possessors of the best plan for the city's future. They did not need to present their plans or their ideas to the people who would either enjoy the benefits or suffer the consequences of their proposals. No, they needed only to impress the bureaucrats or the people in positions of power. It all seemed to me so self-serving. But I was only the bartender.

Curley, any elected official, had to be responsible to the people who elected him.

I would see these well-dressed folks at the Citizens Seminars, and I would also see Curley at lunch at Thompson's Spa on Newspaper Row. This was a lunchroom just down School Street from Old City Hall; if you went down School Street and took a left on Washington, you would come right to it. Curley would sit on a stool at the long counter running the length of the place. He was having a tough time: he was not as well dressed, and his face and jaw were taut. That's my recollection.

I was working in John Karp's meat market on Devine Way when I heard the news that Mayor Curley's son had died, and that his daughter, hearing the news over the phone, died of the shock. It was a sad time for Curley; the pope called to console him. I remember hearing a priest saying he had gone to the wake of one of the children, and told the mayor that the Blessed Aloysius had died at fourteen, and Curley took comfort from it. I wondered if Curley really had. Aloysius Gonzaga actually died at twenty-three. I don't know much about Aloysius, but what I had heard was that someone asked him what he would do if he were told he had only ten minutes to live. He said he would continue playing tennis, as that is what he was supposed to be doing.

Curley continued doing what he was supposed to be doing. Gertrude Dennis told me about a woman who came to the door on the Jamaicaway one morning. The woman was disheveled and looked as though she had been drinking. Gertrude wondered whether she should call the police. The woman said she wanted to talk to the governor. Once you are governor in Massachusetts, you are always the governor. The woman was insistent.

At the top of the stairs the governor appeared. "What is this?" he asked as he came down. He gave the woman a royal greeting, opening the doors to his library and taking her inside. He closed the doors and they talked. Then the library door opened, and the woman emerged with Curley. She was now fully restored. "Thank you, governor. It's nice to see you." And she looked at Mrs. Curley as though Gertrude were the intruder. Gertrude was amazed at the woman's transformation—now fully confident, delighted to be reassured that she had a fine, personal relationship with Governor Curley as he escorted her to the front door.

He explained to Gertrude, after closing the door: "That woman has no place else in this world to go to make a complaint. She has problems. All we have to do is give her an audience. Be patient, listen." Curley no longer could dispense jobs or patronage, but he could give this woman a few dollars for her troubles, and more important, he could listen to her troubles and take them seriously. When she left, she was much cheered by his kindness. She had a very good story to share for years to come. I have heard such stories frequently.

I don't think politics can be appreciated without understanding the personal motives and activities of political leaders. Why do they stay at it? Why do they choose it in the first place? I think there's a basic recognition that this kind of public service is worthwhile no matter what the cost. And this sense of its value grows with experience. The point is underscored by the fact that few would agree with my assessment. They may think that the politician is on an ego trip, or the politician has base motives, psychological or otherwise, for selfish gain or self-enrichment in some way. So the politician who stays the course soon realizes that it will just have to be enough that he himself knows what he has done. We know that Churchill likened politics to war (more exhilarating, he said; in war you can be killed but once); the father of Themistocles of ancient Athens took his son to the beach to show him the old galleys, forsaken and cast about on the shore. This, his father warned, is "how the people behave themselves toward their leaders when they have at last no further use of them."

Fortunately, Themistocles disregarded his father's advice and committed himself to public service. He rebuilt the fleet in time to save Athens from the Persian assault. And ultimately his father's early, unheeded warning was fulfilled. Themistocles was ostracized by the people he had served so well. But it had been worthwhile, especially to the Athenians who had ostracized him. Without him the Persians would have destroyed them.

It is something of a cliché, but what Benjamin Franklin said in 1787, when asked what the men at the Philadelphia convention had created, is still true: a republic, if you can keep it. And certainly it is easier to perpetuate the republic with elected officials

Two originals—James Michael Curley and the Mona Lisa. (Courtesy Boston Public Library)

like Curley than with the self-appointed oligarchy, the aristocrats or the opinion molders who can buy or bully their way to influence.

We do not look as favorably on politicians of our own day as on those who have braved the political tumult of their own day. And none did so more boldly, daringly, and colorfully than James Michael Curley. His life affirms the idea that the political struggle is a worthy undertaking.

What I don't understand, though I suspect few share my perplexity, is why someone would think that the pursuit of material gain will ever result in a sense of having made a contribution to the world. Surely such a person would look back and say, "I've spent my whole life in pursuit of material things, and I regret that I did not give greater emphasis to other avenues." The Reverend Robert Drinan, S.J., onetime Boston College Law School dean and a former congressman, spoke of a man who rued his choice of the pursuit of material things so that he never did anything else. His life, as he looked back on it, was empty.

I was a student at Boston College Law School when Curley died in 1958. I persuaded my friend Ken Joyce, who had a car, to stop by the State House so we could pay our last respects to Curley. Ken had little interest in Curley; in fact, few of my friends did. Ken seemed more interested in the fact that I was interested than he was in Curley's passing. He went with me, I think, out of kindness to me. But what of the 100,000 others who lined up to say farewell? Most had not come because Curley was larger than life, but because in some small way he had made their own lives better. "He got my child a bed in a hospital," one old man said as he waited in line. "My husband lost his job and Curley gave him another." "He got me an apartment in a housing project after we were evicted from our home," another man said. These were the only people, a Boston politician said, who were Curley's real friends.

This connection they felt—it was not the relationship of peasants to their feudal baron, as the muckraking journalists and the Goo-Goos insisted—no, it was the connection of men and women with their government on a very personal basis. Curley understood this on the most fundamental level.

It is an extraordinary tribute to Curley that so many would, for more than half a century, see him, so close-up, with all his imperfections laid bare for all to see, as a man worthy of their steady political loyalty and personal affection.

Some years after Curley's death, Gertrude Dennis Curley and her son spoke of Curley's insistence that it be known that he was grateful for the life he had lived. No one should feel bad about any of the adversity that had befallen him. It was a grand life. He was grateful for it.

A CURLEY CHRONOLOGY

1864 Sarah Clancy, age twelve, and Michael Curley, age fourteen, arrive in Boston from Ireland.

1870 Sarah Clancy and Michael Curley marry, live at 28 Northampton Street.

1872 John Curley, first son of Sarah and Michael, is born.

1874 Sarah and Michael's second son, James, born November 20.

1879 Michael Curley, third son of Sarah and Michael, born; dies 1881. James Curley attends Yeoman Primary School.

1884 Michael Curley dies (age thirty-four) lifting 400-pound curbstone. James Curley goes to work in Gale's Drug Store.

1885 Curley attends Dearborn Grammar School.

1889 Upon completing ninth grade at Dearborn School, Curley goes to work at New England Piano Company.

1897 Curley runs unsuccessfully for Boston Common Council; finishes fourth in field of eleven.

1898 Curley again unsuccessful in race for Common Council.

1899 Curley is elected to Boston Common Council on November 14, finishing second out of nine candidates in ward caucus.

1900 Curley takes seat in Boston Common Council in January.

1902 Curley founds Tammany Club on Hampden Street. Is elected to Massachusetts State Legislature. Takes Civil Service exam for constituent on December 2.

1903 Curley arrested for taking Civil Service exam on February 25 and convicted of fraud April 3. Sentenced to sixty days in Charles Street Jail on November 2. Wins primary nomination for Board of Aldermen on November 19.

1904 Curley begins term in Charles Street Jail on November 7; renominated for Board of Aldermen, 2,238–1,048, on November 17.

1905 Curley released from Charles Street Jail on January 6.

1906 Curley marries Mary Emelda Herlihy on June 27 at St. James Rectory.

1907 James M. Curley Jr. born.

1908 Mary D. Curley born.

1909 Curley is elected to new Boston City Council.

1910 Curley is elected to U.S. Congress from Roxbury/Dorchester/South Boston. Dorothea Curley born.

1912 Curley is reelected to U.S. Congress.

1913 Paul G. Curley born.

1914 Curley is elected mayor of Boston on January 13, beating Thomas Kenny, 43,262–37,522.

1915 Leo F. Curley born. Curleys move into elegant home at 350 Jamaicaway, with shamrocks carved into the shutters.

1917 Andrew Peters defeats Curley on December 18, 37,923–28,848. (James Gallivan comes in third, with 19,427 votes.)

1918 Legislature bars mayor of Boston from serving consecutive terms.

1919 George J. Curley born.

1921 Mary Curley gives birth to twins, John and Joseph. Sarah Curley dies (age sixty-nine). Curley beats John Murphy for mayor, 74,261–71,791, on December 13.

1922 Curley is inaugurated for second mayoral term at Mechanics Hall. Twin sons, John and Joseph, die.

1923 Francis X. Curley born.

1924 Alvan Fuller defeats Curley for governor, 641,000–482,000.

1925 Dorothea Curley dies (age fourteen) in January.

1929 Curley defeats Frederick Mansfield for mayor of Boston, 117,084–96,626, on November 5.

1930 Curley is inaugurated to third term as mayor on January 6. Mary Curley dies on June 10.

1931 James Michael Curley Jr. (age twenty-four), a student at Harvard Law School, dies on January 9. Curley and surviving family members visit Europe. The Mary E. Curley School in Jamaica Plain opens in September.

1932 Curley campaigns for Franklin D. Roosevelt, attends Democratic Convention as delegate from Puerto Rico.

1934 Curley is elected governor of Massachusetts with 736,000 votes to Gaspar Griswold Bacon's 627,000 and Frank Goodwin's 94,000. His term runs 1935–1937.

1935 Mary Curley marries Edward Donnelly in June.

1936 Henry Cabot Lodge Jr. defeats Curley for U.S. Senate, 875,000–732,000; Thomas O'Brien receives 131,000 votes.

1937 Curley marries Gertrude Marion Dennis at St. Mary's Chapel at Boston College on his last day as governor, January 7. On November 2 the *Boston Post* endorses Maurice Tobin for mayor, quoting Cardinal O'Connell on honest men in politics. Tobin wins.

1938 With Curley's power waning, the Legislature in May allows mayors to be reelected. Leverett Saltonstall defeats Curley for governor, 733,000–641,000, on November 8.

1941 Maurice Tobin defeats Curley for mayor, 125,786–116,430; Joseph Lee receives 19,186 votes.

1942 Curley is elected to U.S. Congress from Cambridge/East Boston/ Charlestown district.

1944 Curley is reelected to U.S. Congress.

1945 Paul G. Curley dies (age thirty-two) on October 14. Curley is diagnosed with diabetes. On November 7 he is elected mayor of Boston, receiving 111,824 votes to John Kerrigan's 60,413 and Arthur Reilly's 46,135. Later that month Curley goes on trial in Washington, D.C., for mail fraud.

1946 Curley is convicted of mail fraud on January 18.

1947 Curley begins serving his sentence at Danbury Penitentiary on June 26. On November 26 he is released, having been pardoned by President Truman.

1949 On November 8 John B. Hynes defeats Curley for mayor, 137,930–126,000. Joseph Dinneen, a Boston journalist, publishes *The Purple Shamrock.*

1950 Mary (age forty-two) and Leo Curley (age thirty-five) both die on February 11.

1951 In the mayoral primary on September 25, John Hynes receives 108,414 votes, Curley 77,268, others 17,000. Curley suspends his campaign. On November 6 Hynes receives 154,206 votes, Curley 76,354.

1955 September 27 primary results: John Hynes, 50,957; John E. Powers, 36,407; James Michael Curley, 24,209; Chester Dolan, 18,551.

1956 Edwin O'Connor publishes *The Last Hurrah.* Curley sells his Jamaicaway home to the Oblate Fathers.

1957 Curley publishes his memoir, *I'd Do it Again.*

1958 John Ford's film version of *The Last Hurrah,* starring Spencer Tracy, premieres; Curley dies November 12 at Boston City Hospital (age eighty-four).

1970 George Curley dies (age fifty-one).

1980 Lloyd Lillie's statues of Curley are unveiled by Mayor Kevin White near Faneuil Hall.

1988 George Robert White Fund purchases Curley home, donates it to City of Boston.

1991 *The American Experience* (PBS) broadcasts "The Scandalous Mayor," about James Michael Curley.

1992 Francis Curley, last surviving child of James and Sarah, dies (age sixty-eight). Jack Beatty publishes *The Rascal King.*

1997 Mighty Mighty BossTones record "The Rascal King," an homage to Curley.

A CURLEY BIBLIOGRAPHY

The standard biographies of James Michael Curley are Joseph Dinneen's *The Purple Shamrock* (New York: W. W. Norton, 1949), and Jack Beatty's *The Rascal King: The Life and Times of James Michael Curley, 1874–1958* (Reading, Mass.: Addison-Wesley, 1992). Dinneen's is an authorized biography of a curious kind— the Boston journalist had covered Curley for thirty years, and not always favorably. Curley once sued him for libel. But Dinneen pledged to let Curley tell his story, and in *The Purple Shamrock*, Curley did. Beatty's *The Rascal King,* a more recent and less sympathetic take, has considerably more documentation.

After the success of Edwin O'Connor's *The Last Hurrah* (Boston: Little, Brown, 1956), Curley decided to write his own life story, *I'd Do It Again: A Record of All My Uproarious Years* (Englewood Cliffs, N.J.: Prentice-Hall, 1957), which follows very closely the account Dinneen gave in *The Purple Shamrock.* O'Connor's novel is one of the best novels ever written about American politics; John Ford made it into a film in 1958, with Spencer Tracy playing Skeffington, the Curley character. In 1977 a television remake starring Carroll O'Connor was nominated for three Emmys.

Dicky Barrett and Joe Gittleman from Boston's punk and ska band, The Mighty Mighty Bosstones, also immortalized Curley in their 1997 song "The Rascal King." The song's chorus, "The last hurrah? Nah, I'd do it again," captures Curley's feisty, swaggering belligerence.

Charles H. Trout, *Boston, the Great Depression, and the New Deal* (New York: Oxford University Press, 1977), is a terrific study of Boston politics during Curley's last decade of real dominance. Unfortunately, Professor Trout's ambition to write a biography of Curley has not been fulfilled.

Edmund B. Sullivan, with Barry Mushlin and Robert Colt, turned his collection of Curley memorabilia into a nice book, *Campaigning with James Michael Curley* (Hanover, Mass.: Christopher Publishing House, 2000).

The Curley papers at the College of the Holy Cross in Worcester, Mass., consist mainly of newspaper clippings. The Boston newspapers are a great source for Curley's life and career.

INDEX

Page references given in *italics* refer to illustrations or material contained in their captions.

ABOUT THE AUTHOR

WILLIAM M. BULGER was first elected to the Massachusetts House of Representatives in 1960, inspired in large measure by the political career of James Michael Curley. Elected to the state senate in 1970, Bulger served as senate president for eighteen years, until his appointment by a Republican governor to lead the University of Massachusetts. His first book, *While the Music Lasts*, is a memoir of his life in politics. Bulger lives in South Boston. He and his wife Mary have nine children and thirty-one grandchildren.

ABOUT THE EDITOR

ROBERT J. ALLISON is chairman of the history department of Suffolk University in Boston and teaches courses in American Constitutional history and the history of Boston at Harvard Extension School. He is the author of *A Short History of Boston, The Boston Tea Party, The Boston Massacre, A Short History of Cape Cod,* and other books. He lives in South Boston.

LaVergne, TN USA
05 April 2011
222910LV00006B/4/P